MUSCLE CAR
CLASSICS

MUSCLE CAR
CLASSICS

BY THE AUTO EDITORS OF CONSUMER GUIDE®

Publications International, Ltd.

Louis Weber, CEO
Publications International, Ltd.
7373 North Cicero Avenue
Lincolnwood, Illinois 60712

ISBN-13: 978-1-4127-7658-5
ISBN-10: 1-4127-7658-9

Manufactured in China.

8 7 6 5 4 3 2 1

Library of Congress Control Number: 2008931665

Credits

Photography:
The editors would like to thank the following people and organizations for supplying the photography that made this book possible. They are listed below, along with the page number(s) of their photos.

Roger Barnes: 91; **Joe Bohovic:** 117; **Jeff Cohn:** 31; **Mark Garcia:** 95; **Thomas Glatch:** 45; **Sam Griffith:** 39, 51, 97, 109, 125; **Jerry Heasley:** 19; **Brandon Hemphill:** 9, 65; **Bud Juneau:** 57; **Milton Kieft:** 17; **Dan Lyons:** 23, 107, 119; **Vince Manocchi:** 27, 37, 47, 61, 77; **Roger Mattingly:** 43; **Doug Mitchel:** 11, 15, 49, 59, 67, 73, 75, 81, 89, 93, 99, 103, 127; **Mike Mueller:** 41, 101; **Jeff Rose:** 53; **Tom Salter:** 111, 113; **Tom Shaw:** 83; **Gary Smith:** 55; **Mike Spenner:** 25; **Alex Steinberg:** 87; **David Temple:** 29; **Rithea Tep:** 121; **Phil Toy:** 33, 69, 71; **W. C. Waymack:** 13, 21, 79, 115, 123; **Nicky Wright:** 35, 63, 85, 105

Back Cover: Sam Griffith; Doug Mitchel; Mike Mueller

Owners:
Special thanks to the owners of the cars featured in this book for their cooperation. Their names and the page numbers for their vehicles follow.

Mike Abbott: 89; **Roger Augustine:** 107; **Dennis A. Barnes:** 125; **William C. Bartels:** 65; **Jerry and Carol Buczkowski:** 35; **Stephen R. Campbell:** 29; **Tim Carie:** 77; **Chicago Car Exchange:** 67; **Classic Auto Showplace:** 111, 113; **John Cook:** 81; **Dr. Randy and Mrs. Freda Cooper:** 37; **Garry Day:** 79; **Richard Douglas:** 123; **Bill Draper:** Back cover, 109; **Ray and Gil Elias:** 23; **Gil Espinosa:** 47; **David M. Gabay:** 119; **Gil Garcia:** 33; **Alden Graber:** 11; **Denny Guest:** 15; **Wayne Hartye:** 117; **Brad and Barb Hillick:** 95, 121; **Clarence Hudinski:** 87; **Jeff Hyosaka:** 71; **Charles M. Kerr:** 127; **Ken Kettell:** 13; **Gerald King:** 63; **Richard P. Lambert:** 99; **Jim Lee:** 61; **Michael Leone, Sr.:** 73; **James Lojewski:** 51; **Larry G. Maisel:** 21; **George Maniates:** 83; **Browney L. Mascow:** 85; **Craig P. Mentzer:** 97; **Mr. and Mrs. Richard D. Miller:** Back cover, 41; **Michael Morocco:** 57; **Ronald S. Mroz:** 43; **Vince Muniga:** 55; **MyHotCars.com:** 69; **D. R. Ogsberger:** 53; **Bob Painter:** 17; **Andrew Petersen:** Back cover, 75; **Pat Price:** 27; **Rick Robinson/Northwest Auto Sales:** 9; **Jeff Ruppert:** 103; **Steve Schappaugh:** 91; **Darryl Schleger, M.D.:** 93; **Tom Schlitter:** 19; **Gary Schneider:** 59; **Marvin O. Smith:** 115; **Nate Studer:** 45; **Brian Thomason:** 25; **Craig Tornow:** 31; **John Vincent:** 49; **Barry Waddell:** 101; **Richard Witek:** 39; **Stephen Witmer:** 105

Our appreciation to the historical archives and media services groups of Chrysler, LLC and General Motors Corporation.

CONTENTS

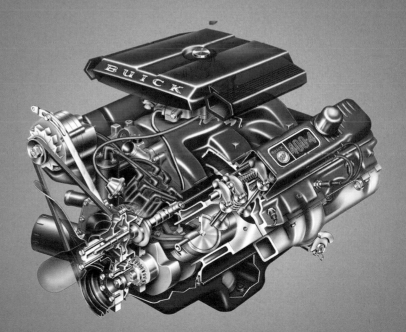

FOREWORD

Pipes and stripes. Four-barrels and four-speeds. Scoops and spoilers. Redlines and raised white letters. These are just a few of the tricks American automakers used to transform their mainstream models into the mean muscle machines that are so fondly remembered today. The muscle car era of the Sixties and early Seventies had its roots in the postwar Detroit horsepower race. It peaked in 1970, when every major American carmaker offered a 340-450-hp super car. High insurance rates, rising gas prices, and increasing government regulation quickly made these factory hot rods obsolete. But their "in-your-face" visuals, pin-you-in-your-seat performance, and the ardent culture that developed around them left a lasting imprint on the automotive landscape. If the lore of muscle cars is out of proportion to their actual numbers, that merely underscores their impact. By the strictest definition, a muscle car is a rear-wheel-drive midsize two-door coupe or sedan with a powerful V-8 engine. *Muscle Car Classics* recognizes, however, that any worthwhile treatment of the subject must go beyond such a confining interpretation. What really matters is a car's use of high power to break away from ordinary transportation. So here you'll find not only GTOs and GTXs, but Camaros and Javelins, Shelby Mustangs and 'Cudas, Galaxies and Impalas. Like the machines themselves, muscle car advertising evolved over time. Early ads highlighted selling points like floor shifters, engine and suspension parts, and race-track prowess. These themes remained important as the era progressed, but scoops, emblems, credibility on the street, and even the artistic presentation of the car itself gained in stature as the muscle car matured. *Muscle Car Classics* mates a selection of the period's most memorable ads with stunning color photography to present a fast-paced journey through this fascinating age.

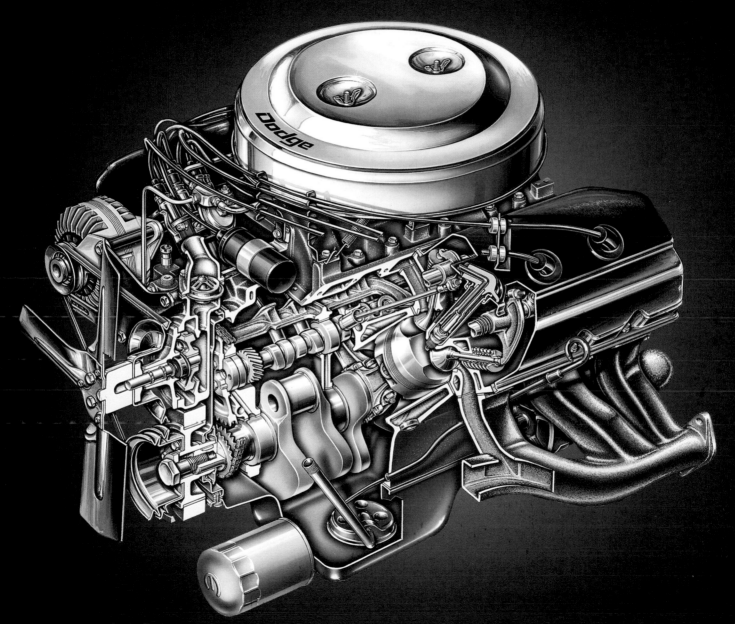

IT FEELS GOOD, LOOKS BETTER and GOES GREAT!

Take any one of Chevy's five '61 Impalas, add either the new 409-cubic-inch V8 or the 348-cubic-inch job and a four-speed floor-mounted stick, wrap the whole thing in special trim that sets it apart from any other car on the street, and man, you have an Impala Super Sport! Every detail of this new Chevrolet package is custom made for young men on the move. This is the kind of car the insiders mean when they say <u>Chevy</u>, the kind that can only be appreciated by a man who understands, wants, and won't settle for less than REAL driving excitement.

Here are the ingredients of the Impala Super Sport kit* • Special Super Sport trim, inside and out • Instrument Panel Pad • Special wheel covers • Power brakes and power steering • Choice of five power teams: 305 hp. with 4-speed Synchro-Mesh or heavy-duty Powerglide. 340 hp. with 4-speed only. 350 hp. with 4-speed only. 360 hp. with 4-speed only • Heavy-duty springs and shocks • Sintered metallic brake linings • 7,000-RPM Tach • 8.00 x 14 narrow band whitewalls • Chevrolet Division of General Motors, Detroit 2, Michigan.

*Optional at extra cost, as a <u>complete</u> kit only.

CHEVROLET

Impala

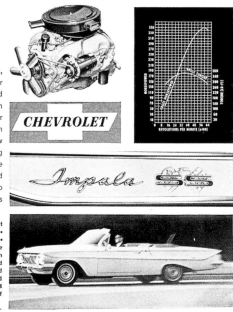

1961
Chevrolet Impala SS

Chevrolet's Impala debuted for 1958 as a top-of-the-line showboat. In mid-1961, Chevy raised the stakes when it delivered a combination punch with the introduction of the Super Sport package and the soon-to-be-famous 409 engine. The $53.80 SS package was ordered on just 453 Impalas that year; most were coupes, but a handful of convertibles also received the option. Special SS equipment included unique body trim, simulated knock-off spinner wheel covers, power steering and brakes, heavy-duty shocks and springs, and a steering-column-mounted tach. Only 142 409s were installed that first year, but they set the stage for the Super Sport mystique. Rated at 360 horsepower and a whopping 409 pound-feet of torque, the hot V-8 could launch an Impala through the quarter-mile in 15.8 seconds.

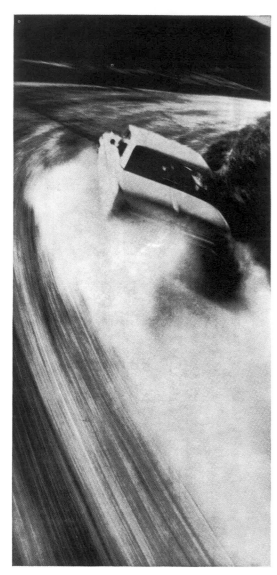

500/XL:
everything but
an afterburner!

Don't pop the clutch on the 405-horsepower version of the Galaxie 500/XL unless you're sure you've got a good bite. Those are big, hairy-legged horses and they can kick gravel and chunks of road a country mile. This stampede is on tap every second...even while you are burbling through town as quiet as a wisp of fog. This top-of-the-line engine is only part of the Galaxie power picture, however. There are four other performance-proved V-8's to choose from. Any one of the top four match up with a smooth four-cog box, or you can get the ease of Cruise-O-Matic on the three smaller ones. Either way you have a console-mounted gear selector inches away from your right hand, and Ford bolts your selection into the smoothest shell that ever whooshed down the pike. Ford craft doesn't stop here, though. Form-fitting bucket seats brace you for fast road work, rear seats are smoothly contoured, and there are seven special interior trims to please your eye . . . when you have time to look at them. Spend an hour with a Galaxie 500/XL on any stretch of road ...it brings out the driver in just about everybody. Your Ford Dealer has the keys to this convincer. A PRODUCT OF
About that afterburner— (Ford)
who needs one? MOTOR COMPANY

Liveliest of the
Lively Ones from
FORD

1962
Ford Galaxie

Ford answered Chevy's 409 and Chrysler's Max Wedge 413 by boring out its 390 V-8 to 406 cubic inches for 1962. Called the Thunderbird 406 High-Performance V-8, and available only in that year's facelifted Galaxie, it signaled a fresh performance push for the blue-oval brigade. The complete 406 package cost $379.70 and required a four-speed manual gearbox and 15-inch tires. Also included were heavy-duty shocks and springs, fade-resistant drum brakes, a larger fuel line, a heavier clutch, stabilizer bar, and a high-capacity radiator. Breathing through the standard four-barrel carb, the 406 was rated at 385 hp. With the Super High Performance Tri-Power, it wore three Holley two-barrel carbs and belted out 405 horses and 448 lb-ft of torque. Quarter-mile times in the mid-15s were the rule with either version.

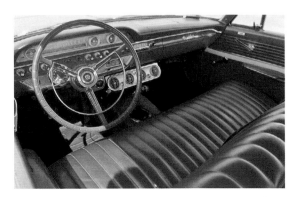

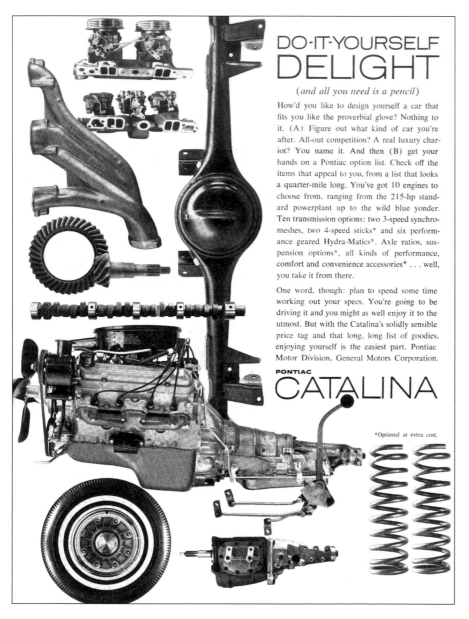

DO-IT-YOURSELF DELIGHT

(and all you need is a pencil)

How'd you like to design yourself a car that fits you like the proverbial glove? Nothing to it. (A) Figure out what kind of car you're after. All-out competition? A real luxury chariot? You name it. And then (B) get your hands on a Pontiac option list. Check off the items that appeal to you, from a list that looks a quarter-mile long. You've got 10 engines to choose from, ranging from the 215-hp standard powerplant up to the wild blue yonder. Ten transmission options: two 3-speed synchromeshes, two 4-speed sticks* and six performance geared Hydra-Matics*. Axle ratios, suspension options*, all kinds of performance, comfort and convenience accessories* . . . well, you take it from there.

One word, though: plan to spend some time working out your specs. You're going to be driving it and you might as well enjoy it to the utmost. But with the Catalina's solidly sensible price tag and that long, long list of goodies, enjoying yourself is the easiest part. Pontiac Motor Division, General Motors Corporation.

PONTIAC
CATALINA

*Optional at extra cost.

1962
Pontiac Grand Prix

Pontiac hardtop coupes, including Catalinas and the new top-line Grand Prix, got a crisp restyle and a new convertible-inspired roofline for 1962. The first Grand Prix was a tastefully dechromed Catalina hardtop that also was outfitted with bucket seats, a tachometer, and a console. The new car helped define the personal-luxury field, and sales of 30,195 made it a hit. The hottest '62 Ponchos packed the SD 421 that was officially rated at 405 horsepower, but in reality the output was closer to 460. Though street legal, these were race-ready engines, with four-bolt mains, forged rods and crank, solid lifters, and high-flow heads. *Motor Trend* ran a Super Duty 421 Catalina to 60 mph in a mere 5.4 seconds, blasting through the quarter-mile in just 13.9 seconds at 107 mph.

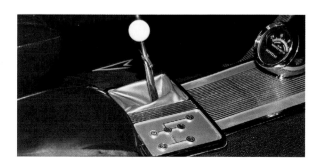

Jim Thornton and Herman Mozer (979) coming off the line in S/SA class.

Some days you win

Mozer and Al Eckstrand in final run for Top Stock Eliminator title.

Some days you lose

The fortunes on the straight and narrow warpath change as quickly as the gears in the go-box! Today you tear 'em up. Tomorrow is another day. Your machine has got to be mean . . . you've got to be good . . . and you've got to come out of the hole with more togetherness than Amos and Andy! That's the drama of the drag strip, man and machine.

That's why more than 100,000 buffs bulged the track at Indy for the NHRA's big showdown—the world championships.

And what a showdown! On Saturday, Jim Thornton in a '63 Dodge downed his Ramcharger teammate, Herman Mozer, on his

way to royalty in the Super Stock Automatic Class. Next day, running for the meet's most coveted honor—Top Stock Eliminator —Mozer turned the tables and gave Thornton the thumb. But the event was far from over. Mozer still had to face the present "Mr. Eliminator," Al Eckstrand in Lawman, another specially equipped '63 Dodge. And another winner is defeated. Mozer edged him by 1/100th of a second with an e.t. of 12.22.

Some days you win. Some days you lose. That's what keeps the quarter-mile jaunt so interesting. But have you noticed? When a Dodge loses these days . . . it's to another Dodge.

Hot Dodge

DODGE DIVISION ★ CHRYSLER MOTORS CORPORATION

1963
Dodge 330

The 1963 Dodge "Ramcharger" 426 V-8 was Chrysler's knee-jerk response to the escalation of the cubic-inch war. Immodestly billed as the "hottest performing power plant to come off a production line," this "Max Wedge" design was the next step up from the 413 V-8 of 1962. Dodge rated the Ramcharger V-8 at 415 horsepower with the standard 11.0:1 compression or 425 ponies with the optional 13.5:1 compression ratio. The odd styling of the 1962 Dodges was toned down for '63, and the wheelbase of standard-size models grew three inches to 119. Hardcore drag racers preferred the cheap, lightweight 330 two-door sedan shown here, but the "Ramcharger" was also available in flashier, more-upscale models, such as the Polara 500 two-door hardtop.

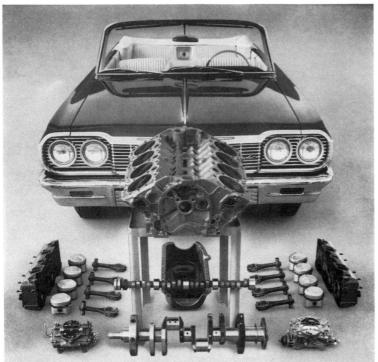

if YOU LIKE PLAYING WITH BLOCKS, TRY THIS. With Chevrolet's Turbo-Fire 409 V8* block you can build to great heights. Say, 340 hp. 400 hp. Or, with the ingredients shown here, 425 hp. All three use the same block. Looks like the Rock of Gibraltar with 409 cubic inches of tunneling punched in it.

For the 425-hp 409 we add all those lovingly machined, cast and forged items above. Twin 4-barrel carburetors. Impact-extruded pistons. Forged steel connecting rods and five-main-bearing crankshaft. Cast alloy iron camshaft. And two heads fitted with lightweight valves. Mechanical valve lifters. Along with things we didn't show—header-type exhaust manifolds, dual exhausts, special clutch and heavy-duty radiator and suspension, among others. For the tamer 340- and 400-hp 409's, we use tamer bits and pieces here and there.

You can tuck a 425-hp Turbo-Fire 409 V8 into any '64 Chevrolet Biscayne, Bel Air, Impala or Impala Super Sport. And choose low gear ratios of 2.56:1 or 2.20:1 with the 4-speed all-synchro shift*. With the 2.20:1 gear ratio you can get 4.11:1 or 4.56:1 Positraction High Performance axle ratios*. Isn't playing with blocks fun?... Chevrolet Division of General Motors, Detroit, Michigan.   *Optional at extra cost

CHEVROLET

1964
Chevrolet Impala SS

Full-size Chevrolets adopted a larger, more formal look for 1964 as the new mid-size Chevelle targeted the youth market. Chevy's full-size Super Sport was promoted to a distinct Impala series rather than just an option package. The SS had new wheel discs with a tri-bar motif, and swirl-patterned trim appeared in the bodyside moldings, on the instrument panel, and on the rear cove. Though available with a six, most SS '64 Impalas were built with a V-8. Buyers could choose from a pair of 283s, three 327s, and burly 409s in 340-, 400-, and 425-horsepower versions; the first could be paired with Powerglide automatic, while the other two were four-speed only. Impala SS sales rose to 185,325. But 409 orders plunged to 8864, as speed demons quickly saw the performance potential of the lighter Chevelle.

'64 Fairlane Sports Coupe; it can wear a Cobra kit, too!

1964
Ford Fairlane

Introduced for 1962, Ford's Fairlane was the industry's first true intermediate. Essentially an enlarged Falcon riding a 115.5-inch wheelbase, Fairlane fell between the compact Ford and the full-size Galaxie in size and price. Ford's small-block V-8 engine debuted under the hood of the Fairlane and related Mercury Meteor. The new engine initially displaced 221 cubic inches, but 260- and 289-cubic inch versions quickly appeared. By '64, the Fairlane received its second facelift, and Ford's Total Performance campaign was in full swing. A 427-powered Fairlane Thunderbolt was produced in limited numbers for dragstrip duty. But the top street cars, like this Fairlane 500 Sport Coupe, were powered by a 271-horse version of the 289. Extra horsepower was available at the dealer through Shelby-inspired bolt-on Cobra kits.

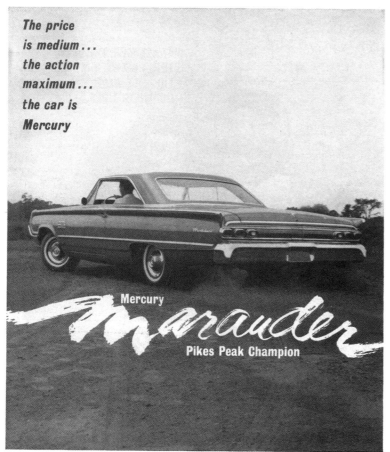

The price
is medium...
the action
maximum...
the car is
Mercury

Mercury
Marauder

Pikes Peak Champion

The name is the tip-off . . . Marauder! This is an action car. Looks it. Acts it. A 390 cu. in. V-8 is standard. Optional engines range up to an 8-barrel, 427 cu. in. V-8 — the newest edition of the engine that set a new world's stock-car record in the most recent Pikes Peak Climb. Choose from six Marauder models — 2-door or 4-door hardtops. Or, if you prefer, the same performance is available in Mercurys with Breezeway Design (the rear window opens for ventilation). See both at your Mercury dealer's. LINCOLN-MERCURY DIVISION (Ford) MOTOR COMPANY

'64 Mercury
No finer car in the medium-price field

1964
Mercury Marauder

Full-size Mercurys received an attractive pointed nose with an "electric shaver" grille and other styling tweaks for 1964, but the "Super Marauder" 427 was unchanged after its 1963 debut. In base form, the engine used a Holley four-barrel mounted atop an aluminum intake manifold to produce 410 horsepower and 476 lb-ft of torque. Checking the "427 8V Hi-Perf" option box brought twin four-barrel Holleys and 11.5:1 compression. A floor-mounted four-speed was mandatory with the dual-quad 427, and just 42 Marauders were so equipped. Like their fastback Ford cousins, these Mercs were formidable on stock car tracks, winning seven USAC-series races and five on the NASCAR circuit. Famed racer Parnelli Jones wheeled 427-powered Marauders to first place finishes at the Pikes Peak hillclimbs in 1963 and 1964.

1964
Plymouth Sport Fury

Plymouths were virtual carryovers for 1964, though a new grille and taillamps were added, while two-door hardtops got a new roof. Bucket seats and a console again graced the topline Sport Fury, but the driver faced a fresh dashboard with four gauges in a brushed metal panel. And, for the first time, a four-speed manual trans-mission could be ordered. The Fury's console-mounted tachometer was a $50 extra, and its location made it hard to read from the driver's seat. Chrysler's new 426 Hemi was tearing up stock car tracks and dragstrips across the country, but it wasn't yet available for the street in regular production Mopars. Plymouth's hottest "over-the-counter" engine was the 426 Max Wedge Stage III Super Stock V-8. It was conservatively rated at 425 horsepower but wasn't well-suited to daily driver duty.

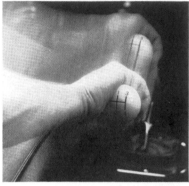

GTO is for kicking up the kind of storm that others just talk up.

Standard Equipment: engine: 389-cu. in. Pontiac with 1-4BBL; bhp—325 @ 4800; torque—428 lb-ft @ 3200 rpm/dual-exhaust system/3-speed stick with Hurst shifter/heavy-duty clutch/heavy-duty springs, shocks, stabilizer bar/special 7.50 x 14 red-line high-speed nylon cord tires (rayon cord whitewalls optional at no extra cost)/14 x 6JK wide-rim wheels/high-capacity radiator / declutching fan / high-capacity battery (66 plate, 61 amp. hr.)/chromed air cleaner, rocker covers, oil filler cap/bucket seats/standard axle ratio 3.23:1 (3.08, 3.36*, 3.55* to 1 available on special order at no extra cost). **And some of our extra-cost Performance Options:** engine: 389-cu. in. Pontiac with 3-2BBL (Code #809); bhp—348 @ 4900;

torque—428 lb-ft @ 3600; 3.55:1 axle ratio standard with this engine option/4-speed with Hurst shifter (gear ratios 2.56:1, 1.91:1, 1.48:1, 1.00:1, and 2.64:1 reverse)/2-speed automatic with 2.20:1 torque converter/Safe-T-Track limited-slip differential (Code #701)/3.90:1 axle ratio available on special order with metallic brake linings, heavy-duty radiator and Safe-T-Track/handling kit—20:1 quick steering and extra-firm-control heavy-duty shocks (Code #612)/high-performance full transistor (breakerless) ignition (Code #671)/tachometer (Code #452)/custom sports steering wheel (Code #524)/exhaust splitters (Dealer installed)/wire wheel discs (Dealer installed)/custom wheel discs, with spinner and brake cooling holes (Code #521)/console (Code #601).

*Available only with heavy-duty options at slight additional charge.

the GTO makers—Pontiac

PONTIAC MOTOR DIVISION • GENERAL MOTORS CORPORATION

1964
Pontiac Tempest GTO

This is it. The 1964 Pontiac Tempest GTO was the first modern mass-produced production automobile to put big-cube power in a midsize body—a formula that defined the true muscle car. Pontiac circumvented a GM rule prohibiting intermediates from having V-8s more than 330 cubic inches by making its 389 V-8 part of an option package for the new Tempest, a ploy that didn't require corporate approval. The name Gran Turismo Omologato was borrowed from the Ferrari 250 GTO. The term defines a production grand touring machine homologated, or sanctioned, to race. The GTO's 389 made 325 horsepower with the standard four-barrel carb. An optional Tri-Power version used three two-barrels and was rated at 348 hp. Pontiac hoped to sell a modest 5000 '64 GTOs; final production totaled 32,450.

G.T. 350

Precise control takes on a new meaning behind the wheel of Shelby American's new Mustang GT-350! The complete suspension system has been re-designed to comply with a computer plotted geometry that allows the GT-350 to stick like nothing you've ever driven. Reflex quick steering, Koni shocks, and Goodyear 130 mph "Blue Dots" let you pick your exact line . . . and stick to it! No use mentioning the GT-350's 306 hp Cobra hi-riser 289 or the competition proven disc brakes until you've actually sampled a few corners at speed. The most complex blind apex closing radius bend becomes the expert driver's challenge instead of an exercise in frustration. When you go down to test the GT-350, ask the salesman to bring your present car along for comparison . . . you won't believe it! Suggested list price $4547.00

for more information write Dept S, Shelby American, 6501 W. Imperial Hwy., Los Angeles, California 90009

1965
Shelby G.T. 350

Not willing to stop at creating a new market for sporty compacts with the Mustang, Ford also wanted to enhance its performance image and beat Corvette in SCCA racing in the bargain. Carroll Shelby, who had changed the gentle AC roadster into the Ferrari-taming Cobra, was called in to add some kick to the Mustang. Ford sent semi-finished 2+2 fastbacks with the High Performance 289-cubic inch engine to Shelby's shop in Venice, California. Shelby hiked the horsepower from 271 to 306. Acceleration was exciting: 0-60 mph came in 6.5 seconds and the quarter mile in 14.9 at 95 mph. The suspension was modified to harness the power, and engine bay bracing stiffened the front structure. Body modifications included a fiberglass hood with a functional scoop. Inside, a spare-tire shelf replaced the back seat.

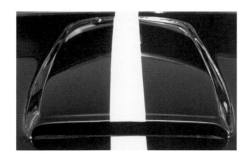

There are Buicks that would rattle your faith
in the established order of sporting machinery.
The Skylark GS, for one.

Notch-back seats that convert into semi-buckets
are standard. Bucket seats are available.

A tachometer is available.

The standard engine. Bhp—325 @
4400. Torque—445 lb-ft @ 2800.

More engine. Extra cost. Bhp—340
@ 4600. Torque—445 lb-ft @ 3200.
Carburetion—Quadrajet 4BBL.

Floor-shift all-synchro 3-speed
standard. Automatic and close-
ratio 4-speed are available.

Chromed-steel 14-inch wheels are available. Choice of 7.75 x 14 red-line or whitewall
tires at no extra cost. Axle ratios: 2.78, 2.93, 3.36, 3.55, 3.90. 4.30:1 (special order).
Positive Traction is included with all performance axles, at extra cost.

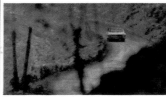

Heavy-duty springs, shocks, stabilizer bar, and
frame are standard. Metallic brake linings and a rear
stabilizer bar are available, dealer installed.

The following safety
equipment is standard on
all Buicks: 2-speed electric
wipers and windshield washer;
padded dash; padded sun
visors; back-up lights;
shatter-resistant rear-view
mirror; outside rear-view
mirror; and front and rear
seat belts (which we sure
wish you'd buckle).

**1966 Buick.
The tuned car.**

1966
Buick Gran Sport

A total restyling of all four General Motors intermediates was ordained for 1966. Like its corporate siblings, the Skylark Gran Sport was new all over. Buick signaled its commitment to the muscle car market by elevating the Gran Sport from a Skylark option package to its very own series of two-door sedans, hardtops, and convertibles. Distinguishing the Gran Sport were a blacked-out grille, new GS emblems, nonfunctional rear-facing hood scoops, and simulated front fender vents. The base 401-cubic-inch "Wildcat 445" had 325 horsepower, but a hotter 340-horse version was added during the model year. Dual exhausts and a heavy-duty suspension were standard with either engine. The GS did not prove as popular as its corporate kin. Buick built 106,217 Skylarks for 1966, of which only 13,816 were Gran Sports.

1966
Chevrolet Impala SS

The legendary 409 was replaced by the new Mark IV 396-cubic-inch "big-block" V-8 during 1965. The 396 returned for 1966, but the big news was a bored-out variation: the Turbo-Jet 427. The new engine was available only in Corvettes and full-size Chevys. Any member of the big-car line could be had with one of two versions: a hydraulic-lifter model with 390 horsepower, or a solid-lifter version with 425. Only 5143 full-size models were ordered with a 427. The sports model remained the Impala SS, but by 1966, midsize performance cars were ruling the street. Chevrolet's major emphasis this year was the extension of 1965's Caprice Custom Sedan into an entire series. The expanded Caprice lineup stole a lot of thunder from the Impala SS, and full-size performance was fading quickly at Chevy and across the industry.

CHARGER

... new leader of the Dodge Rebellion.

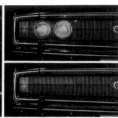

You never had it so luxurious, sports. Bucket seats, center console with padded armrest and full carpeting are just a few standard '66 Dodge Charger comfort features.

Dodge Charger's tach is no add-on afterthought. It's right up next to the speedometer, where it belongs. The swivel clock mounted on the console is optional.

Charger's "now-you-see-'em, now-you-don't" headlights look great no matter what position they are in, and move into place automatically.

This beautiful new bomb comes from the drawing board to your driveway with all the excitement left in. It's Dodge Charger, and it's loaded. With fresh ideas, eye-tempting styling, explosive performance. "What a handsome home for a Hemi!" you say? We thought you would—so a big, bad 426 Street Hemi is optional. In a package deal with a heavy-duty suspension— 0.92-inch torsion bars, link-type sway bar, high-rate rear springs and heavy-duty shocks—to keep you firmly in control. Plus 11-inch brakes and 4-ply nylon Blue Streak tires for extra safety. Add to the package with options like a heavy-duty TorqueFlite automatic transmission (set for full-throttle shifts at 5500 rpm) or a competition-type, 4-speed manual gearbox. Check out Charger, the hot new one from Dodge that proves sports cars can also be luxurious.

Cross a sporty-type car and a station wagon, and what happens? Dodge Charger! These handsome rear seats fold down to give you lots of extra luggage space—enough to handle a pair of skiis.

A winner, going away. That's Dodge Charger, the new smoothy. And just as it packs a big punch under the hood up front, you'll find you can pack a big load under that clean, crisply styled rear deck lid. Fold the rear seats down, and you've got about 7½ feet of completely carpeted cargo space.
* YOU HAVE A CHANCE OF WINNING A DODGE CHARGER—REGISTER AT YOUR DODGE DEALER'S.

Dodge Charger

DODGE DIVISION ✶ CHRYSLER MOTORS CORPORATION

1966
Dodge Charger

Fastback rooflines were all the rage in the mid-Sixties, so Dodge dropped a sleek new roof on its midsize Coronet to create the 1966 Charger. The flashy new model cost $417 more than a Coronet 500 hardtop, and part of the deal was a state-of-the-art '60s interior. It had lots of chrome, four bucket seats with folding rear seat-backs, available center consoles front and rear, and full instrumentation that included a 150-mph speedometer and 6000-rpm tach. Hidden headlights and a full-width taillight further spruced up the exterior. A mild-mannered 318-cubic inch V-8 was standard, but 1966 was the year Chrysler's 426 Hemi V-8 came to the streets. A Street Hemi added $877.55 to Charger's $3122 base price and was too wild for most buyers. Of 37,344 Chargers built for '66, only 468 packed a Hemi under the hood.

HOW TO COOK A TIGER

Take one part 335 HP V-8. Chrome plate the rocker covers, oil filler cap, radiator cap, air cleaner cover and dip stick.

Blend high lift cam; bigger carburetor.

Mix in the new 2-way, 3-speed GTA Sport Shift that you can use either manually or let shift itself.

Place the new shift selector between great bucket seats.

Now put on competition type springs and shocks.

Add a heavy-duty stabilizer bar.

Place over low profile 7.75 nylon whitewalls.

Touch off with distinctive GTA medallion and contrasting racing stripe.

Cover with hardtop or 5-ply vinyl convertible top with glass rear window. Serve in any of 15 colors.

This is the new Fairlane GTA. An original Ford recipe that may be tasted at your Ford Dealers . . . Remember--it's a very hot dish!

FAIRLANE

GTA

A PRODUCT OF

Ford

1966
Ford Fairlane

With its 1966 redesign, Ford's Fairlane finally had an engine bay large enough for big-cube power. GT versions had a 335-horse 390-cubic-inch engine and could turn mid-15s at around 90 mph in the quarter-mile. Those numbers didn't cut it against GM and Mopar's hottest midsizers, so Ford produced a small run of 427-powered Fairlanes for dragstrip battle. The 427 was good for 410 horsepower with a single four-barrel, or 425 with dual quads. Also included were a four-speed transmission, front disc brakes, and a 9000-rpm tach. The 427 Fairlane's lift-off fiberglass hood was held down by four NASCAR-style tie-down pins and had a functional air scoop. A production run of at least 50 was required to qualify the car for the NHRA's A/S Super Stock class, and Ford is believed to have built just 57 including the car pictured here.

GTO stands for *Gran Turismo Omologato*. You've probably heard of it. A Pontiac in a saber-toothed tiger skin. The deceptively beautiful body comes in convertible, sports coupe, and hardtop configurations. With pinstriping. On a heavy-duty suspension system that thinks it's married to the ground. Bucket seats and carpeting. Wood-grained dash. Redlines or whitewalls at no extra cost. Chromed 335-hp 4-barrel under the hood. Fully-synchronized 3-speed on the column. Or order a heavy-duty all-synchro 3-speed or 4-speed with Hurst floor shifter. Or 2-speed auto. Or the 360-hp 3 2-BBL. There's a catalog full of options. See if you can get your Pontiac dealer to cough one up. That's the GTO/2+2 performance catalog. You'll recognize it. It vibrates.

Speak softly and carry a GTO

Pontiac Motor Division • General Motors Corporation

1966
Pontiac GTO

Recognizing the GTO's growing popularity, Pontiac promoted it from a Tempest option to a model of its own for 1966. The "Goat" rewarded Pontiac with sales of 96,946 units, the highest one-year total ever attained by a true muscle car. And while all GM midsize cars were restyled for '66, none matched the beauty of the GTO's new Coke-bottle contours. Wheelbase was untouched, and overall length and curb weights changed negligibly. But styling highlights included a graceful new roofline and cool fluted taillamps. The standard hood scoop remained nonfunctional, but Tri-Power engines could get an over-the-counter fresh-air kit, and a few were equipped with the Goat's first factory Ram Air. The four-barrel 389 continued at 335 horsepower. The triple-two-barrel version was rated at 360 horses and cost $113 extra.

Pontiac Motor Division • General Motors Corporation

Standard plumbing: 421 4-BBL, 338 hp. Duals, straight-through mufflers, low-restriction resonators. Chromed low-restriction air cleaner, rocker covers, oil filter cap. 3.08, 3.23 or 3.42 rear axles, all-synchro 3-speed with Hurst. Heavy-duty suspension, buckets, carpeting. Front and rear seat belts an enthusiast will use and appreciate. *Extra-cost plumbing:* 421 Tri-Power, 356 and

376 hp. 4-speed with Hurst, Turbo Hydra-Matic. Extra-large diameter exhaust system, extra-heavy-duty suspension. Transistorized ignition, oil pressure and water temperature gauges, tach. Limited-slip. Heavy-duty radiator, oil cooler and battery, aluminum wheel hubs and drums, 3.73 and 4.11 rear axles and all the other items you'll see in our special GTO/2+2 performance catalog.

Pontiac 2+2. Listen! Did you hear something growl just then?

1966
Pontiac 2+2

Pontiac first offered the 2+2 as a Catalina engine, suspension, and trim group for 1964. For 1966, the 2+2 became a separate model, still based on the Catalina two-door hardtop or convertible. Features included a heavy-duty suspension, with even stiffer springs and shocks available. Buckets and a console were added to the top-line Catalina interior, which could be optioned with a sport steering wheel and instrumentation that included a tach and oil-pressure gauge. Unique exterior features included "2+2" badges, twin-lens taillamps, and chrome bodyside gills. Pontiac's famous eight-lug aluminum wheels were optional. This was the only Poncho with standard 421-cubic-inch power. A 338-horse four-barrel was the base engine. Two tri-power 421s were optional, one with 356 ponies, the other with 376.

1967
Chevrolet Chevelle SS

The Chevelle SS 396 took several steps forward and a couple steps back for '67. Advancements came mainly in road manners and drivability. New lower-profile F70x14 tires helped improve grip and steering response. The Wide Ovals also helped get the most out of the newly available front disc brakes. Accompanying the discs were purposeful-looking 14-inch slotted wheels. Exterior changes were minor, with a slightly reworked bumper and grille and a blackout tail panel. A three-speed manual was again the standard transmission, with a four-speed also available. The two-speed Powerglide automatic returned, but for the first time the three-speed Turbo Hydra-Matic joined the options list. A 325-horsepower version of the 396-cubic inch V-8 was standard, with the L34 upgrade rated at 350.

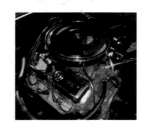

41

super hooded Super Sport SS 427

Gentlemen, we have before us one very special automobile: Chevrolet's new SS 427.

That big bulging hood? We'll level with you. It's there to tell the world that there's something very special underneath: a 427-cubic-inch 385-horsepower Turbo-Jet V8 with porcupine heads, angled valves, dual exhaust and 4-barrel carb.

Special springs, shocks and stabilizer bar are part of the package. So are special markings and red stripe tires.

You can add 4-speaker stereo, front fender lights, set-and-forget air conditioning, special instrumentation, whatever you like. SS 427: just the ticket for the sporting man who likes some room to move around in.

SS 427 Sport Coupe: a swashbuckling new species of Chevrolet

Special markings.   Special suspension standard.   You can add 4 on the floor . . .   or disc brakes up front.   Mark of Excellence.

Chevrolet gives you that sure feeling

CHEVROLET

1967
Chevrolet Impala SS 427

Chevrolet's full-size cars got a voluptuous new "Coke-bottle" shape for 1967. Sporty Impala SS models continued and were supplemented by an extra-special Super Sport model: the SS 427. The package included the 385-horsepower 427 that was available on any full-size 1967 Chevy, stiffer springs and shocks, a front stabilizer bar, and red-stripe tires. Exterior styling features included a unique domed hood with faux air-intake scoops, blacked-out vertical grille bars, and special emblems. Interestingly, the car wore no "Impala" badges. *Car Life* tested a 427-powered Impala that hit 60 mph in 8.4 seconds and ran the quarter-mile in 15.75 seconds at 86.5 mph, decent numbers for a vehicle of this size and heft. Just 2124 SS 427s were produced this year, as enthusiast car-buyer tastes continued their shift to smaller models.

1967
Dodge Coronet R/T

Dodge's midsize Coronet was given handsome new styling for '66 and could be armed with devastating power. The Street Hemi was optional, but to casual observers, a modest "426 Hemi" badge was all that separated it from grandpa's grocery-getter. For 1967, Dodge conjured up the Coronet R/T—for "Road and Track"—as its first comprehensive muscle model. The R/T added enough visual cues to make its meaning clear. There was an exclusive Charger-inspired grille with exposed headlamps, plus modest nonfunctional hood slats and small R/T emblems. Underneath, the R/T was all business: The suspension had heavy-duty everything, and a 375-horse 440 was standard. The only optional engine was the 426 Hemi, again rated at 425 horsepower. Dodge built 9553 R/T hardtops in 1967, along with 628 convertibles.

sedate it ain't

400 CID V-8. Full 115-inch wheelbase. Heavy-duty springs, shock absorbers, shaft. Sway bars, front *and rear*. High-performance axle. Dual exhausts. Beefed-up wheels. White-Line or wide-oval Red-Line tires. Bucket seats. Louvered hood. Higher oil pressure. They're all standard goodies at one modest price. Available also, if you wish—Rocket Rally Pac, UHV ignition, superstock wheels, front disc brakes and the like. Put one into action and you'll agree : 1967 Olds 4-4-2 is the sweetest, neatest, completest anti-boredom bundle on rubber!

OLDS 442 **GM**

ENGINEERED FOR EXCITEMENT...TORONADO-STYLE!

1967
Oldsmobile 4-4-2

Oldsmobile's 4-4-2 came on the scene during 1964 as a "police package" for the midsize F-85/Cutlass that could even be ordered on four-door sedans. Olds refined the idea for 1965, making it an option on two-door coupes, hardtops, and convertibles. In 1967, Olds called its sporty models the "Youngmobiles" and said the 4-4-2 was "the sweetest, neatest, completest anti-boredom bundle on rubber!" All 4-4-2s had a four-barrel 400-cubic-inch V-8 rated at 350 horsepower. An optional W-30 package brought forced-air induction, a hotter cam, and stronger valve springs—but was still rated at 350 horses. *Car and Driver* ran the quarter-mile in 15.8 seconds with a regular 350-hp 4-4-2. *Hot Rod's* W-30 four-speed turned the quarter in 13.9 seconds, while one with the automatic did it in 14.5.

Goldilocks and the two Bears.

The Bear on the right is a stock Belvedere GTX.

That is to say it carries the standard 440 cu. in. V-8, which, aside from being the biggest GT engine in the world, generates 375 hp. and 480 lbs.-ft. of torque through a fast-shifting TorqueFlite automatic and the recommended 3.23-to-1 rear axle.

Said Bear also carries a heavy-duty suspension—including beefed-up torsion bars, ball joints, front stabilizer bar, shocks and rear springs—along with bigger brakes, low-restriction exhausts, a pit-stop gas filler, chromed valve covers, Red Streak tires, wide rims, hood scoops and bucket seats. And this is the *standard* Bear, mind you.

The Bear on the left is also a stock GTX—with a heavy-duty 4-speed gearbox—*and* a few extra-cost options, including the famed Hemi, with 426 cu. in. and 490 lbs.-ft. of torque. It also has our super-duty Sure-Grip differential; not to mention racing stripes and front disc brakes.

So what's the moral? Simply that GTX is one very tempting bowl of porridge. In one form, even Goldilocks can drive it (although you'll recall Goldilocks was a highly adventuresome kind of female). In another form, it's strictly for the "Move over, honey, and let a man drive" set. You know the story: there's bound to be one that's just right. After all, we're out to win you over. '67 Belvedere GTX.

1967
Plymouth GTX

There were plenty of fast Plymouths prior to 1967, but none had the unified performance image pioneered by the Pontiac GTO. Plymouth addressed this for '67 with an executive-class hot rod that leaned a little on the Poncho for its name: GTX. Based on the handsome Belvedere hardtop and convertible, the GTX was dressed up with a special grille and tail panel, simulated hood scoops, and chrome gas cap. Twin racing stripes were optional. The cabin was top-of-the-line, with bucket seats and lots of brightwork. Going fast without fuss was the GTX's mission, so it got Mopar's newly fortified 375-horsepower 440 V-8 as standard. Also included was Chrysler's unassailable three-speed TorqueFlite automatic transmission and a heavy-duty suspension. Some 720 buyers forked over an extra $546 for the mighty Hemi engine.

1968
AMC AMX

After spending the majority of the Sixties resisting the trend toward high-performance cars, American Motors finally jumped on the muscle car bandwagon with the 1968 Javelin and AMX. The Javelin was a four-seat ponycar; the AMX was a short-wheelbase, two-seat "sports car" variant. The AMX's 97-inch wheelbase was one inch shorter than a Corvette's, and its $3245 base price with the standard 225-horsepower 290-cubic-inch V-8 was $1100 less. AMXs had balanced handling as well as good straight-line kick. A 280-horse, 343-cubic-inch V-8 could replace the 290, but most buyers opted for the 315-horse 390. A "Go" package added power front disc brakes, E70x14 tires, Twin-Grip limited-slip differential, and racing stripes. Equipped with the 390, an AMX could run the quarter-mile in 14.8 seconds. Just 6275 '68 AMXs were built.

You wouldn't expect anything to match Corvette's sports car ride and handling.

Bucket seats behind a long, low hood. Bump-smoothing, curve-straightening four-wheel independent suspension. V8s that range from a standard 327 cubic inches up to a 427 that you can order. New full door-glass styling. New Astro Ventilation. More beauty, more excitement than ever. And *still* America's only true production sports car.

But when you drive "The Hugger"... will you be surprised!

Bucket seats behind a long, low hood. A smooth-riding, road-hugging improved suspension system. V8s you can order that start at 327 cubic inches and work their way up to 396. Sleek full door-glass styling, like Corvette. Flow-through Astro Ventilation, like Corvette. Command drive a Camaro . . . Corvette's road-hugging running mate!

Corvette Sting Ray Coupe and running mate, Camaro SS Coupe.

GM
MARK OF EXCELLENCE

Camaro '68 CHEVROLET Corvette

Be smart! Be sure! Buy now at your Chevrolet dealer's.

1968
Chevrolet Camaro

Refinement was the byword for Camaro's second season. Astro-Ventilation, which circulated fresh air through the interior, spelled the demise of the vent windows. And new federal regulations brought on side-marker lights. Super Sport equipment added just $210 to the bottom line and included a heavy-duty suspension and a 285-horsepower 350-cubic inch V-8. Buyers could also get a 396 big block in 325-, 350-, or 375-horse flavors. More tempting to some was the Z/28, which had a 302-cubic-inch V-8 under the hood. The 302 was created by putting the crankshaft from a 283 V-8 into the 327's block to get under the SCCA's 305-cubic-inch limit for its Trans Am road-racing series. The big bore and short stroke let the engine rev to 7200 rpm, and it was conservatively rated at 290 horsepower.

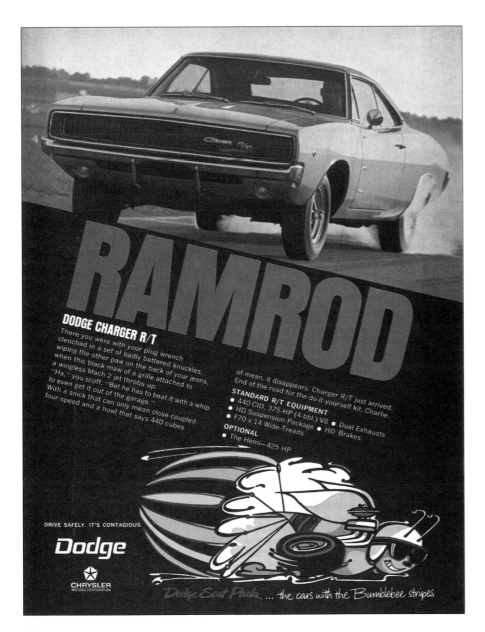

1968
Dodge Charger

A breathtaking, all-new Charger debuted for 1968. Its new hidden-headlamp grille, curvy body, elegant recessed backlight, refined tail, and spare use of chrome represented a styling high point for 60's muscle cars. And in R/T form, its performance justified equal praise. For $3506, the R/T came with the 375-horse 440 Magnum V-8, heavy-duty brakes, R/T handling package, and F70x14 tires. Just 475 Charger R/Ts were ordered with the optional 426 Hemi. With TorqueFlite and standard 3.23:1 gears, *Car and Driver*'s Hemi Charger got to 60 in 6.0 seconds and turned a killer 13.5 seconds at 105 mph in the quarter-mile. For most buyers, the standard 440 Magnum was enough. Manually shifting the TorqueFlite, *Motor Trend* got its 440 Charger to 60 mph in 6.5 seconds, and through the quarter in 14.85 at 95.5 mph.

The hidden persuaders:

ENGINE

Type.............................Rocket V-8
Bore x stroke, inches.........3.87 x 4.25
Displacement, cubic inches..........400
Compression ratio..................10.5-to-1
Bhp............................350° at 4800 rpm
Torque, lb.-ft............440 at 3200 rpm
Carburetion..............................4-bbl.
Exhausts..............................Dual
   Built-in Combustion Control System provides constant carb air temperature.
   Availabilities: Force-Air Induction System. 360 bhp at 5400 rpm. Teams with close-ratio 4-on-the-floor transmission or Turbo Hydra-Matic.
   Cruising package: Includes 400-CID V-8 with 2-bbl. carb, 290 bhp, 9-to-1 compression, Turbo Hydra-Matic, 2.56-to-1 axle.
*325-hp Rocket 400 V-8 with 4-bbl. carb and 10.5-to-1 compression ratio teams with Turbo Hydra-Matic.

DRIVE TRAIN

Transmission.........Fully synchronized, heavy-duty 3-on-the-floor with Hurst Shifter
   Availabilities: 4-on-the-floor (close- or wide-ratio with Hurst Shifter) or Turbo Hydra-Matic floor shift.
Prop shaft.......................Heavy-duty
Axle ratios......2.56-to-1 up to 4.66-to-1
   Availabilities: Heavy-duty axles (H.D. shafts, bearings, differential gears), 3 ratios.

CHASSIS

Suspension.........Heavy-duty. Includes heavy-duty springs and shocks, front and rear stabilizers.
Steering ratio......................24-to-1
Wheels...............Heavy-duty 14-inch with extra-wide rims
Tires................F70x14", Nylon-Cord Wide-Oval Red-Lines

OTHER AVAILABILITIES

Power front disc brakes. UHV Transistorized Ignition. Anti-Spin Differential. Rally Stripes. Rally Pac (clock, tach, engine gauges). Sports console. Custom Sport Steering Wheel. Simulated-wire and Super Stock Wheels. Special wheel discs. Others.

GENERAL

Wheelbase............................112"
Overall length......................201.6"
Overall width..........................76.2"
Overall height........................52.8"
Curb wt. (lb.) Holiday Coupe........3628
Tread............front 59.0", rear 59.0"

SAFETY

All the new GM safety features are standard, including energy-absorbing column, seat belts for all passenger positions.

Olds 4-4-2

Three bucket-seat youngmobile models: Holiday Coupe, Sports Coupe, Convertible.
CARS Magazine names Olds 4-4-2 "Top Performance Car of the Year."

1968
Oldsmobile 4-4-2

Oldsmobile's 4-4-2 entered 1968 with curvaceous new styling and full-series status. Three body styles were available: a pair of coupes (hardtop and pillared) and a convertible. The base powerplant continued to be the 400-cubic-inch Rocket with 10.5:1 compression ratio and a four-barrel carburetor. Manually shifted cars received a 350-horsepower V-8, while those with Turbo Hydra-Matic had to make due with 25 less. The ultimate 4-4-2 carried a potent W-30 air-inducted version rated at 360 horsepower. The 4-4-2 buyer continued to get a lot of heavy-duty equipment, including beefier shocks, springs and sway bars; high performance tires, and wider wheels. A one-year only option was W-36, which brought a vertical rally stripe just behind the front wheels.

The Missing Link.

Until now, there were two distinct types of stock cars.
There was the street stock. And, indeed, it was just that.
Despite the acquisition of big-displacement engines and ferocious nicknames, it was basically a boulevard car. The emphasis was on luxury: expensive interiors, lavish adornments, and lots of brightwork.
Then there was the other type—the Grand National stocker.
You couldn't buy it, and even if you could, your name would have to be Petty or something to get it started on a cold morning.
Nevertheless, it was infinitely attractive—the low silhouette; the super-wide tires; the stovepipe exhausts; the absence of chrome; the Spartan cockpit—sort of brutally good-looking.
Obviously there was a need for a car that combined some of the civilized comforts of the street stock with the integrity of the Grand National type.
So we created the Missing Link.
It's called the Road Runner, and you'd better believe it's one hairy-idling, stiffly-sprung, squat-sitting, wide-tired, de-chromed automobile.
Unlike most stocks, Road Runner doesn't sport an interior of hand-rubbed, fake Ukembeki wood. It doesn't even have Buck Rogers signature-model seats. Like a real stocker, it's all-business inside: a couple of gauges, a big Hurst gear lever and clutch, brake and accelerator pedals. The exterior is similarly functional.
The standard engine is an exclusive high-output version of Plymouth's 383 cu. in. V-8. Optional, and very fitting, is the big 426 Hemi.
The body is a two-door coupe with a hardtop roofline, and it's rigid as only a stocker can be.
The suspension is completely heavy-duty, front and rear.
The only real concession to the boulevard is the addition of a horn, and even that has character. It goes "Beep-Beep!" just like the bird in the cartoons.
Oh yes—and the doors work. On Grand National cars they're welded shut.
. . . the Plymouth win-you-over beat goes on. ♥

Plymouth CHRYSLER MOTORS CORPORATION

1968
Plymouth Road Runner

Muscle cars quickly evolved from mainstream models with expensive special engines to expensive special models with expensive special engines. The youth of America needed an inexpensive mainstream model with an inexpensive special engine. In 1968, Plymouth gave it to them. The Road Runner started as a pillared coupe, the lightest and least-costly iteration of the handsome new Belvedere body. The engine was Mopar's 383-cubic-inch V-8, with heads, manifolds, and numerous other goodies from the big, bad 440 Magnum. The new mill made 335 horses. The interior was bench-seat austere, and the base price was a stingy $2896. The Road Runner became a smash hit. Plymouth forecasted sales of 2500, but buyers snapped up nearly 45,000. Of those, only 1019 had the optional 426 Hemi engine.

The Great One by Pontiac.   **You know the rest of the story.**

1968
Pontiac GTO

When GM redesigned its intermediates for 1968, no division had a tougher act to follow than Pontiac. But talent rose to the challenge and the new GTO emerged as a brilliant blend of beauty and brawn. It sustained the styling leadership of the 1966-67 series, and its performance remained competitive against ever-tougher rivals. Best of all, its aura was intact. A 400-cubic inch V-8 remained standard. The base version gained 15 horsepower to 350, while the HO and Ram Air versions climbed to 360. Midyear, the original Ram Air engine was replaced with the 366-horse Ram Air II. Nothing rivaled the GTO's new Endura bumper, which was molded and color-keyed to form the car's clean new nose. Hidden headlights were new and proved so popular that most people didn't realize they were options.

Try the <u>complete</u> surprise . . . Carroll Shelby's COBRA GT

Carroll Shelby reasons that a *true* GT needs *everything* for high performance pleasure, comfort and safety engineered right in, not just offered as afterthought options. That's why his Cobra GT is a *complete* surprise to those who see it and drive it for the first time. ☐ Surprise number one is style. Subtle changes in grille, hood, sides, rear deck add a fresh, exclusive look. Interior luxury follows through with deep-bucket seats, walnut-grain appliques, front seat center console-armrest, courtesy lights, full instrumentation. ☐ Naturally, you expect performance . . . but the GT 500's Shelby-ized 428 cubic inch V-8 rewrites the performance charts with surprising smoothness. A 302 V-8 is Shelby-prepared for the GT 350. Special wide-path tires. 16-to-1 power steering, modified suspension and adjustable super-duty shocks deliver firm control but with enough velvet to make an all-day trip a pleasure. ☐ Safety features are engineered-in, too. These include an overhead safety bar and inertia-reel shoulder harnesses, impact-absorbing steering wheel, dual braking system. ☐ By engineering his other surprises into the great-to-start-with Mustang, Carroll Shelby's biggest surprise is the small price. ☐ Your Shelby dealer will prove just how big *that* surprise can be.

Shelby COBRA GT 350/500   POWER BY Ford

1968
Shelby GT 500KR

Racing legend Carroll Shelby's first production Mustangs debuted in 1965 as barely tamed thoroughbreds that were more at home on the track than the street. By 1968, they had morphed into more civilized "grand-touring" machines that blended aggressive performance with upscale comfort. Shelby dressed up the stock '68 Mustang with special fiberglass nose panels, fiberglass hood with working scoops and vents, bodyside intakes, and a spoilered tail with sequential turn signals lifted from the '65 Thunderbird. A padded roll bar, improved gauges, and woodgrain trim was added to the other-wise stock Mustang interior. At midyear, the GT 500's 360-horse 428 V-8 was replaced by a Cobra Jet, which, though factory-rated at "just" 335 hp, actually put out closer to 400. With that, the car adopted the GT 500KR (for King of the Road) tag.

A Rambler that does the quarter mile in 14.3.

American Motors and Hurst have collaborated on the custom-built SC/Rambler.

It's a limited production car; only 500 units are planned at this time.

Enough to qualify the SC/Rambler for stock classes in drag racing.

The price is $2,998! Which is very little money when you see what it buys.

1. 390 cubic inch AMX V-8 Engine.
2. 4-speed all-synchromesh close-ratio transmission.
3. Special Hurst 4-speed shift linkage with T-handle.
4. A Sun tach mounted on the steering column.
5. Dual Exhaust system with special-tone mufflers and chrome extensions.
6. Functional Hood Scoop for cold-air induction.
7. Twin-Grip differential.
8. 10½" diameter clutch.
9. 3.54:1 axle ratio.
10. Power disc brakes (front).
11. Rear axle torque links.
12. Handling package (heavy-duty front sway bar plus heavy-duty springs and shocks).
13. Heavy-duty cooling system (heavy-duty radiator,

power-flex fan and fan shroud).
14. A 20:1 manual steering ratio.
15. Special application of new Red, White and Blue exterior colors.
16. Two hood Tie-Downs with locking safety pins and cables.
17. Custom Tear-Drop racing mirrors (one each side).
18. Custom Grille.
19. Custom SC/Rambler-Hurst emblem on front fenders/rear panel.
20. Mag styled wheels, 14" x 6", painted specially to complement exterior color scheme.
21. Five E 70 x 14 Goodyear Polyglas™ Wide-Tread tires.
22. Sports steering wheel.
23. Custom-upholstered head restraints in Red, White and Blue vinyl.
24. All-vinyl charcoal seat upholstery with full carpeting.
25. Individually adjustable reclining seats.

There's more, but you get the idea. With this car you could make life miserable for any GTO, Roadrunner, Cobra Jet or Mach 1.

American Motors'/Hurst SC/Rambler

1. Manufacturer's suggested retail price includes all items listed and federal taxes. State and local taxes, if any, and destination charges excluded.

1969
AMC SC/Rambler

AMC followed an age-old hot-rod recipe, stuffed its biggest engine into a compact body, and got help from Hurst Performance Research to create the Rogue-based Hurst SC/Rambler. It appeared in mid-1969 and was sold for that year only. The SC/Rambler, or "Scrambler," borrowed the AMX's 315-horse 390-cubic-inch V-8 and added ram-air induction. The $2998 base price also included a Borg-Warner four-speed with a Hurst shifter, a Twin-Grip differential, Polyglas tires, front-disc brakes, and a Sun 8000-rpm tach. All SC/Ramblers started out as appliance-white hardtops with two-tone mags, racing mirrors, blackout grille and tail panel, Hurst badging, and an exaggerated hood scoop. About two-thirds of the 1512 built had the wild paint scheme shown here; the rest made do with more-subdued rocker panel stripes.

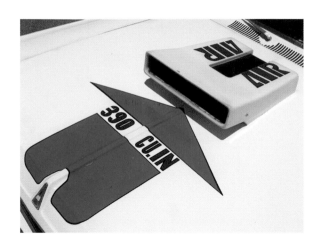

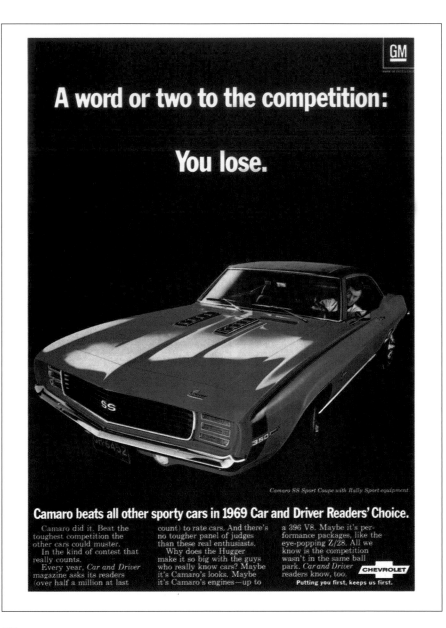

A word or two to the competition:

You lose.

Camaro SS Sport Coupe with Rally Sport equipment

Camaro beats all other sporty cars in 1969 Car and Driver Readers' Choice.

Camaro did it. Beat the toughest competition the other cars could muster.

In the kind of contest that really counts.

Every year, *Car and Driver* magazine asks its readers (over half a million at last count) to rate cars. And there's no tougher panel of judges than these real enthusiasts.

Why does the Hugger make it so big with the guys who really know cars? Maybe it's Camaro's looks. Maybe it's Camaro's engines—up to a 396 V8. Maybe it's performance packages, like the eye-popping Z/28. All we know is the competition wasn't in the same ball park. *Car and Driver* readers know, too.

Putting you first, keeps us first.

1969
Chevrolet Camaro

On occasion, Detroit comes up with a one-year wonder that strikes a chord with its audience. The '69 Camaro was like that. A deft revamp of the 1967-68 body shell created unique styling used just for this season. Good thing the '69s were so interesting. As it turned out, they had to be carried into the 1970 model year when the introduction of the second-generation Camaro was delayed. The most popular enthusiast Camaro was again the Super Sport, which added about $300 to a coupe or convertible and included a 300-horsepower 350-cubic-inch V-8. More than 34,000 Camaros were outfitted in Super Sport trim. Of those, 13,970 were ordered with the big-block 396 V-8. This one eschewed the optional hidden-headlamp Rally Sport package but added rally wheels, "hockey-stick" bodyside stripes, and a vinyl top.

The class bully.

SS 396.

Challenge it.

That's one way to find out what makes the '69 Chevelle SS 396 toughest in its class.

Just check its credentials.

A 396-cubic-inch 325-horse-power V8.

A beefed-up suspension sys-tem poised on 7-inch sport wheels and white lettered wide ovals.

If you want to go the whole route, order the 4-speed, the full instrumentation package, the 350-horsepower mill.

Any way you spec it out, the new SS 396 is a hundred and one percent pure car.

Pick one up at your Chevy dealer's as soon as you can.

Then watch the rest of the class step aside. CHEVROLET

Putting you first, keeps us first.

1969
Chevrolet Chevelle SS

Although the SS 396 Chevelle was muscle for the common man, set up the right way, its performance was distinctly uncommon. After a year as a separate model, the SS 396 was made a $348 option package for '69. SS 396s looked cleaner than ever. The power-bulge hood was still just for show, but more prominent "SS 396" badging and standard five-spoke mag wheels burnished the image. A 325-horsepower version of the 396 was standard, with 350- and 375-horse versions optional. Chevy not only sold a record 86,307 SS 396s in '69, but more than 9000—an all-time high—were ordered with the 375-horsepower L78. Traction problems and a sloppy four-speed linkage gave stock examples deceptively modest ETs. But few muscle cars responded so well to simple modifications, showing that common doesn't always mean average.

The Sleeper Awakes

1969
Chevrolet Nova SS

Some street racers weren't attention seekers. They got their kicks by humbling flashy, high-buck muscle cars, shutting them down in an ambush of speed and stealth. The Nova SS 396 seemed ideal for such duty. Chevy redesigned its compact for '68, but the look was still tame. The chassis was shared with the Camaro, so big blocks finally fit. Sure enough, the 396 V-8 appeared as a Super Sport option partway through '68. For 1969, the 396 was back in 350-horsepower tune and as a 375-horse L78. This was the hoodlum Nova. SS badges, black-accented grille and tail, and simulated hood air intakes marked the exterior, but nothing shouted supercar. Still, all stealthiness seemed to dissolve with the L78. What the "396" numerals on the fender suggested, the racket of solid lifters and the rumble from the dual exhausts confirmed.

6,000 RPM
FOR LESS THAN $3,000

DART SWINGER 340

Play your cards right, and three G's can put you in a whole lot of car this year. Dart Swinger 340. Newest member of the Dodge Scat Pack. You don't make it on looks alone. 340 cubes of high-winding, 4-barrel V8. A 4-speed Hurst on the floor to keep things moving. All the other credentials are in order. Just check at right. Then check with your Dodge Dealer. Especially about the price.

STANDARD DART SWINGER 340 EQUIPMENT

- 340-cubic-inch 4-bbl. V8
- 4-speed full synchromesh with Hurst shifter
- Heavy-duty suspension
- Dual exhausts
- D70x14 wide-tread tires
- Dart Swinger bumblebee stripes
- Performance hood with die-cast louvers
- 3.23 axle ratio. 3.55 and 3.91 are optional ratios, with Sure Grip differential.

Dodge Scat Pack ... the cars with the *Bumblebee* stripes

1969
Dodge Dart

If Dodge had an engine to rival the energetic small-block Chevy, it was the eager, free-revving 340-cubic inch V-8. Underrated at 275 horsepower, the 340 could power a light-weight Dart to easy mid-14-second quarter-miles—much to the embarrassment of many a big-block supercar. The 340 was standard in the showcase GT Sport trim level, which included bumblebee tail stripes to mark its membership in the new Dodge Scat Pack collection of performance cars. Optional in the GTS was the 383 rated at a realistic 300 horsepower. Taking a cue from the low-buck successes of the Super Bee and Plymouth Road Runner, Dodge added a new budget performance model to the '69 Dart lineup: the Swinger 340. The 383 was exclusive to the GTS, but the upstart Swinger 340 still outsold its more expensive sibling by almost 10,000 units.

1969
Dodge Super Bee

In mid 1969, Chrysler engineers used some good ol' hot-rodding savvy to create one of the muscle era's most intoxicating cars. They took Mopar's fine 375-horse 440 Magnum and treated it to the time-honored hop-up of more carburetion, replacing the single Carter quad with three Holley two-barrels on an Edelbrock Hi-Riser manifold. Hemi valve springs, a hotter cam, magnafluxed connecting rods, and other fortifications helped boost horsepower to 390. A Hurst-shifted four-speed and 4.10:1 rear were standard. TorqueFlite was optional, but disc brakes and air conditioning were not allowed. The 440 Six Pack package added $463 to the cost of a Super Bee—about $400 less than the optional 426 Hemi. Included were plain steel wheels adorned only by chrome lug nuts and a wild lift-off fiberglass hood.

Ford-Powered Double A Fuel Dragster.

Here's what happens when you put a 10.5:1 cr, 429 cid, V-8 in a Mustang...

Boss 429!

The cars in Ford's Performance Corner have to be winners. So we called all our competition engineers together and built a new road car—Boss 429.

We start with the same 429 block casting the NASCAR boys get. We four-bolt the mains, put in a forged steel crank, forged rods with ⅜ inch bolts, and forged pop-up pistons. She redlines at six and a half grand.

On top we went a little ape. Aluminum heads mated to the deck, huge canted valves that open way up on hydraulic lifters and forged rocker arms that just don't bend. Ports are oversized, chambers are crescent shaped. Manually controlled Ram-Air induction comes on strong via a 735 cfm 4-barrel Holley and aluminum high riser manifold. It all adds up to 375 horsepower, and that's understating it considerably.

We put the power on the ground through a 4-speed, heavy-duty box and a 3.9-to-1 Daytona type locker axle driving 7-inch chrome-styled-steel wheels carrying F60 x 15 Polyglas belted wide ones. The car stays where you point it with high-rate springs and shocks, plus heavy-duty roll bars fore and aft. Staggered shocks handle the torque problem. Power front discs do the stopping; power steering directs all the action.

What's the model? Thought you'd never ask! Mustang SportsRoof with dual racing mirrors, bright exhaust extensions, tach, front spoiler and full instrumentation. Another Going Thing. You'll find it at your Ford Dealer's Performance Corner. Or at the strip.

For your free copy of Ford's 1969 Performance Buyer's Digest, write: Performance Digest, Department HR, P.O. Box 1000, Dearborn, Michigan 48121

MUSTANG *Ford*

1969
Ford Mustang Boss 429

The Boss 429 was born of Ford's need to qualify 500 examples of its new racing engine for NASCAR. But instead of putting production units in the midsize Torinos it ran in stock-car racing, Ford offered the engines in its restyled '69 Mustang fastback. It was a serious mill: four-bolt mains, a forged steel crankshaft, and big port, staggered-valve aluminum heads with crescent-shaped combustion chambers. Boss 429s were refreshingly clean outside, with simple decals, hood scoop, front spoiler, and Magnum 500 wheels. Air conditioning and automatic transmission were forbidden. This was the costliest non-Shelby Mustang. The superspeedway-bound 429 thrived on high revs—bad news for standing-start acceleration. As a result, quarter-mile performance fell short of other big-block specialty cars, but mid-range punch was awesome.

GRAND SLAM!
Torino wins 1968 NASCAR, USAC and ARCA championships.

And Cobra's coming on for more!

Torino started strong by taking the first five places in the first race it entered, the 1968 Riverside 500. Torino finished strong, too. Specially modified Torinos won all three stock car racing crowns. Boss drivers Dave Pearson, A. J. Foyt and Benny Parsons did a lot of hard charging to get us there.

What's all this got to do with you and our new street machine? Plenty. Something as quick and mean as Cobra doesn't happen until you do a batch of triple-crown-winning Torinos. Cars that go fast grow slowly! With Better Ideas born in the heat and hustle of stock car racing.

Take a good look at Cobra by Ford. Standard 428 CID 4-barrel V-8 rated conservatively at 335 horses. (The *largest* standard engine in any car in its class.) Competition suspension with staggered rear shocks

to soak up the 440 lbs-ft of torque that beast above throws out. Wide-tread belted F70 x 14 grabbers mounted on 6-inch rims. Four-on-the-floor, all-synchro box, exposed hood lock pins.

If you really want to get down and dirty about it, put in the 428 CID Cobra Jet V-8 with through-the-hood Ram-Air induction, power front discs and Traction-Lok differential. The only surprise left in your life is the price—very low.

Go to your Ford Dealer's Performance Corner and test-drive a Cobra. Run it up to five grand and you'll know we're telling it like it is.

COBRA *Ford*

For your free copy of Ford's 1969 Performance Buyer's Digest, write: Performance Digest, Department SG, P.O. Box 1000, Dearborn, Michigan 48121

For a full color Cobra decal, send 25¢ in coin to: Cobra, P. O. Box 1000, Dearborn, Mich. 48121

1969
Ford Torino Cobra

Ford jumped on the budget-muscle bandwagon in 1969. The subject was a dressed-down Torino hardtop or SportsRoof fastback with the grille blacked out and minimal exterior ornamentation; about the only clue to the car's true nature were the standard hood pins, small Cobra emblems, and "428" badges that gave away the standard 428-cubic-inch Cobra Jet V-8. The $3200 base price also included a four-speed manual, with automatic a $37 option. Although Ford rated the Cobra Jet at 335 horsepower, its true output was closer to 400. The optional Ram Air induction system cost $144 and used a functional hood scoop. These CJ-R engines retained the 335-horse rating but were stronger than the regular mill. Finally, Ford had a midsize street machine that lived up to the reputations of its drag-strip and oval-track siblings.

1969
Mercury Cyclone CJ

Like its cousin the Ford Torino, Mercury's Cyclone was an intermediate that rode a platform dating back to the original 1960 Falcon compact. The main performance model was the Cyclone CJ. As the name implied, the 428 Cobra Jet was standard, with the CJ-R (Ram Air) optional. The base price was $3224, and included a competition handling package, F70 fiberglass-belted tires, and a black-out grille. A Drag Pak option replaced the standard 3.50:1 gears with 3.91:1 or 4.30:1 cogs, and added "Le-Mans" connecting rods and an engine oil cooler. The Ram Air induction option included the functional hood scoop and hood lock pins. Torquey and foolproof with automatic transmission, these were Mercury's finest street racers, with consistent ETs in the low 14s at 100 mph.

1969
Oldsmobile Hurst/Olds

Oldsmobile was the automaker most closely associated with Hurst. Jack "Doc" Watson, Hurst's head of research, had supervised the creation and production of the mighty '68 Hurst/Olds 4-4-2. The Hurst/Olds was back for '69, but no longer was it low-key in silver and black. Bold "Firefrost Gold" striping now accented its white paint. On the hood was a flamboyant dual-snout scoop more efficient at feeding the engine than the under-bumper Force-Air inlets found on other 4-4-2s. The decklid held an enormous airfoil that supplied additional downforce. The Hurst/Olds again used a 455-cubic-inch V-8 that was outfitted with W-30 goodies. Dubbed W-46, the mill was rated at 380 horsepower. A performance-modified automatic transmission with a console-shifted Hurst Dual-Gate was mandatory. Production totaled less than 1000.

CUDA 340 STORMS THE QUARTER   RIGHT IN FRONT OF NHRA AND EVERYBODY

PLYMOUTH TELLS IT LIKE IT IS.

For a copy of Plymouth's wild new high-performance car catalog, send 50¢ to Supercars, P.O. Box 7749, Dept. R, Detroit, Michigan 48207.

1969

Plymouth 'Cuda

For 1969, Plymouth committed itself to Barracuda performance hook, line, and, unfortunately, sinker. It coined the 'Cuda name to identify a new enthusiast package for fastback and hardtop models with the 340- or 383-cubic-inch engine, but the baddest 'Cuda of all came in on a wave that crested midyear. Feeling pressure from big-block rivals, Plymouth and Hurst/Campbell managed to shoehorn the 375-horse 440 into a batch of 'Cuda fastbacks and coupes. On the plus side, Plymouth now had bragging rights to the largest-displacement pony car of the day. ETs were down, sometimes into the high 13s. But there were problems. Power steering and brakes weren't available because the engine bay was too crowded to allow the hardware to fit, which only aggravated the car's nose-heavy clumsiness in the twisties.

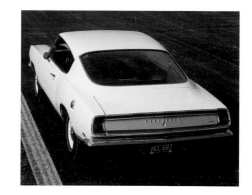

PLYMOUTH TELLS IT LIKE IT IS.

1969
Plymouth GTX

Entering its third season, GTX styling was tidied up in detail, while the basic package of heavy-duty suspension/shocks/brakes, chrome engine trim, and an unsilenced air cleaner was retained. The Super Commando 440 remained standard, with the Hemi optional; the Road Runner's 440+6 engine was not a GTX offering. New options included the Air Grabber hood. It was not a hood scoop, but rather an air intake that allowed cool outside air to reach the engine. A "Track Pak" added a four-speed with Hurst shifter, seven-blade viscous-drive fan, dual-breaker distributor, and a Sure-Grip rear end. Plymouth's promotional illustrations were the period's most evocative, conveying in caricature the power and personality of its muscle cars. By 1969, the artwork had evolved to the style so wonderfully represented here.

The Graduate.

We'll grant you two wheels are better than none. But look what happens when Firebird swoops onto the scene. If it's our 400 version.

You won't believe how this one handles. Don't let the smoothness fool you. New rear axle, new load rates on our multi-leaf rear springs and a set of sticky wide-ovals (mounted on 7-inch rims) put new shine on Firebird's cornering reputation. A 400-cubic-inch, Quadra-jet V-8 attached to a 3-speed, heavy-duty transmission, stirred by a Hurst, is your standard power setup. But there's also our two-scoop Ram Air IV that you can order with a 4-speed hand shifter or with 3-speed Turbo Hydra-matic, if you just tell your dealer.

Obviously, all that genius is below decks. Topside, Firebird comes on with all-new looks. Inside, new comfort. With wider, more heavily padded bucket seats wrapped in Pontiac's own woven vinyl. Also, an all-new highly readable instrument panel.

Hood tach, front disc brakes, variable-ratio power steering, polyglas-cord, wide-tread rubber . . . all that great Pontiac stuff . . . will practically let you build your own Firebird . . . if you want to.

And that's a liberal education in itself.

Firebird 400 by Pontiac

The Wide-Track Family for '69: Grand Prix, Bonneville, Brougham, Executive, Catalina, GTO, LeMans, Custom S, Tempest and Firebird. Pontiac Motor Division.

88

1969
Pontiac Firebird 400

After less than two years on the market, Firebirds enjoyed a facelift. Change was most evident in the Endura plastic front end, where the split grille was narrower and quad headlamps sat in separate compartments. Slim, fluted taillamps continued, but in a revised rear panel. Firebird 400 remained the muscular version, with its 330-horsepower 400-cubic-inch V-8. Also included were twin hood scoops, special handling suspension, and chrome engine dress-up components. The top engine option was the 345-horse Ram Air IV 400. The hood-mounted tach was an $85 extra. In March 1969, the $725 Trans Am Performance and Appearance package for Firebird 400s quietly slipped into the lineup. It was an inauspicious beginning for a car that would soon become Pontiac's performance flagship.

The Judge. It's justice man, justice.

If that sounds strong, it's meant to. Because there are a lot of so-called performancy cars roaming the streets.

But there's simply no fooling with The Judge. Exhibit A: a standard, 366-horse, 400-cube Ram Air V-8 with Quadra-jet carburetor. Exhibit B: the 370-horse, 400-cubic-inch Ram Air IV V-8 which can be ordered on The Judge.

The verdict's the same whether that power's coupled to a 3-speed, fully synched, manual gearbox. Or ordered with a close-ratio, Hurst-stirred 4-speed or Turbo Hydra-matic.

Got the picture, gang? Just be on the lookout for a 60"

airfoil, big, black, fiber-glass belted tires, custom black grille, steel, mag-type wheels and blue-red-yellow striping.

And never let it be said Pontiac didn' give you fair notice.

THE JUDGE

Four color pictures, specs, book jackets and decals are yours for 30¢ (50¢ outside U.S.A.). Write to: '69 Wide-Tracks, P.O. Box 888F, 196 Wide-Track Blvd., Pontiac, Michigan 48056.

1969
Pontiac GTO Judge

Under most circumstances, a judge commands respect. But society in 1969 was increasingly irreverent toward establishment figures, and "Here comes da judge!" quickly went from a sardonic catchphrase on TV's *Laugh-In* to a staple of the American lexicon. In naming the newest GTO incarnation "The Judge," Pontiac seemed to be saying: "This car has authority, but like the Road Runner and its ilk, it doesn't take itself too seriously." Rather than an econo-muscle Goat, the Judge was a $332 option package for the GTO hardtop or convertible. Standard was the 366-horse Ram Air III evolution of the GTO's 400-cubic-inch V-8. This judge did not hold court only in a somber black robe, as vivid colors were offered, and a rear-deck spoiler, blackout grille, and Judge decals decorated the body.

Uncommon...
you might even call it rare!

Sitting still . . . the Shelby looks invincible. But just turn it on and let it out and you'll see how that long low racy styling dares anything else to come close.

When racing expert Carroll Shelby designs a car this way you don't expect him to build very many. He doesn't.

The Shelby is a true elegant, luxury, high performance car. It offers the responsiveness of a sports car with the comfort and luxury of a $15,000 Grand Turismo machine.

Carroll Shelby has adapted the famous ram air Cobra Jet 428 engine to his own GT 500. The GT 350 on the other hand, is fitted with a 351 CID engine for sporty handling and excitement. In '69 Shelby delivers a firm, heavy duty suspension, advanced design, agile handling, crisp front disc braking, and a host of engineering refinements and safety features you expect to find in a true-road-car.

If you are tired of the hum-drum try the unique 1969 Shelby. A test drive will convince you. At most Shelby performance centers Jan. 31; some may have it already.

Shelby GT 350/500

Visit your local Shelby Performance Dealer

POWER BY *Ford*

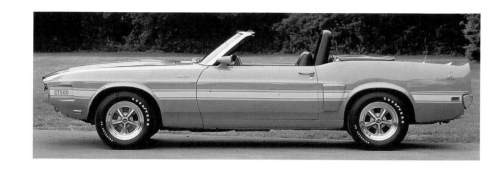

1969
Shelby GT 500

From the front, at least, the 1969 Shelby GTs looked less like concurrent Ford Mustangs than any that had been made since 1965, when former racing legend Carroll Shelby started putting his touch on Ford's "pony car." That's ironic, given that the '69 Shelbys were more the work of the Ford Motor Company than they were of "Ol' Shel." Ford had gradually taken over production from Shelby after the lease on his California plant expired. The GT continued to be offered in two ways. One was a small-block GT 350 (now with a 351-cubic-inch V-8), the other a GT 500 with a 428 Cobra Jet engine. The 428 continued to be advertised at a stout 335 horsepower, as it had been in 1968, but some estimates thought this was a bit conservative. Production came to 3150 for the year, with only 335 being GT 500 convertibles.

A Javelin for the track.

On this page you see a basic Javelin specially-prepared and modified for Trans-American Road Racing.

It's been clocked at 175 mph, goes from 0 to 60 in under 5 seconds, does the quarter-mile in under 11 seconds.

One of the country's top performance writers, Karl Ludvigsen, said in a recent article: "Hopefully, American Motors will see fit to sell an exact street equivalent of its Trans-Am Javelin, because it could be one of the nicest in a nice class of cars."

Which brings us to the Javelin on the opposite page.

This year, we're producing a limited number of Javelins in racing red-white-and-blue.

We couldn't make it an *exact* street equivalent. That's illegal.

We have, however, put in standard equipment that's optional in most other cars.

It has a 390 engine. Ram-air hood. Dual exhaust system. Heavy-duty engine cooling. Twin-grip differential.

A Javelin for the road.

4-speed close-ratio gear box with Hurst shifter. Power disc brakes in front. Heavy-duty springs and shocks. Front and rear spoilers. F70 x 14 tires with raised letters. 140 mph speedometer and tachometer.

Now, if the racer's a little too much for you, there's the Javelin that started our sports car craze in the first place.

We've put in standard highback bucket seats and redesigned the instrument panel.

We've also added a lot of new options.

Like corduroy upholstery trim in five colors, leather trim in three. Landau-style vinyl roof. New style rally and accent stripes.

And a lot of other things that can make the Javelin look and act just as racy as you want it to.

American Motors

1970
AMC Javelin

AMC's pony car, the Javelin, received a minor facelift for 1970, highlighted by a "twin-venturi" grille, revised hood, and reshuffled trim. Inside, there were high-back bucket seats and a new dashboard. AMC offered a limited number of Javelins finished in a red, white, and blue paint scheme like that worn by the Javelin Trans-Am racers. A 325-horsepower 390 V-8 was found under the Ram-Air hood. Other features included a four-speed manual transmission, twin-grip rear end, and unique front and rear spoilers. Only about 100 were built during September and October 1969. AMC lured team owner Roger Penske and his star driver Mark Donohue over from Chevrolet for the 1970 Trans-Am season. To capitalize on this partnership, AMC issued a run of 2501 Mark Donohue Javelin SSTs, complete with a decal of Donohue's signature on its Donohue-designed rear spoiler.

Introducing the Rebel "Machine."

Standing before you is the car you've always wanted.

And, if you like everything about it, except for the paint job, which admittedly looks startling, you can order the car painted in the color of your choice.

You may be wondering why a company like American Motors would paint a car red, white and blue.

And that's what we keep asking ourselves: Why would a company like American Motors paint a car red, white and blue?

But we have nothing to be embarrassed about under the hood, which is all you should be concerned about.

The Machine has a 390 CID engine as standard equipment and develops a horsepower the equivalent of 340 horses all pulling in unison, which is no mean feat.

Next, and this will be particularly impressive to those people who have buried their heads in hot rod magazines since they were old enough to say "zoom . . . zoom . . . lookee it's a car," the Machine has a 4-speed all-synchromesh close-ratio transmission with special Hurst shift linkage and a 3.54:1 standard rear axle ratio (or an optional 3.91:1).

To feed air to your engine, and it will be your engine once you buy the car, we have bolted on a ram-air hood scoop. And in the hood scoop, we mounted a tach that's lighted and registers 8000 rpm's.

Heavy-duty shocks and springs raise the rear end a bit and give the Machine, a raked, just mowed the lawn look.

And our dual exhaust system uses special low back pressure mufflers and larger exhaust pipes.

We will make the description of the rest of the Machine's features mercifully short. Front and rear sway bars, high-back bucket seats, 15 inch tires with raised white letters, mag styled steel wheels, power disc brakes, and racing stripes that glow in the dark.

Incidentally, if you have delusions of entering the Daytona 500 with the Machine, or challenging people at random, the Machine is not that fast. You should know that.

For instance, it is not as fast on the getaway as a 427 Corvette, or a Hemi, but it is faster on the getaway than a Volkswagen, a slow freight train, and your old man's Cadillac.

In short, in order to fully make up your mind about the Machine, you will have to see it in person at your American Motors dealer.

And when you're introduced to it, a simple "How do you do?," "Nice meeting you," or something friendly like "How are your pipes?," will suffice.

Up with The Rebel Machine

For a set of four "Up with the Rebel Machine" decals send 25¢ and your name and address to: Machine Decal Offer, American Motors Sales Corporation, 14250 Plymouth Road, Detroit, Michigan 48232.

1970
AMC Rebel Machine

The 1969 SC/Rambler proved to be a one-year wonder. For '70, AMC introduced a performance version of its intermediate Rebel two-door hardtop. Dubbed "The Machine" and initially resplendent in red, white, and blue paint—later all standard Rebel colors were available—the new car was powered by an exclusive 340-horse-power version of AMC's 390-cubic-inch V-8. A Hurst-shifted four-speed was standard, while a Borg-Warner automatic with a console shifter was optional. Machines also came with a functional ram-air hood scoop and had dual exhaust with low back-pressure mufflers. The heavy-duty suspension used station-wagon rear springs, which elevated the tail and helped account for the raked look. *Road Test* magazine pushed their Machine to a 14.57 quarter-mile at 92.77 mph.

THE MACHINE

Buick's GSX.
A limited edition.

• 455-4 Engine (350 Horsepower) • Tachometer-hood mounted • Special Rallye Steering Wheel • Power Front Disc Brakes • 4-speed Manual Transmission • 3.42 axle ratio with Positive Traction Differential • G60-15 Billboard Wide Oval Tires • Special Front Stabilizer Bar • Front and Rear Spoilers • Bucket Seats (Black) • Heavy duty front & rear shocks • Rear Stabilizer Bar • Rear Control Arms & Bushings • Firm Ride Rear Springs • GSX Ornamentation.

Another light-your-fire car from Buick.

GM
MARK OF EXCELLENCE

BUICK MOTOR DIVISION

1970
Buick GSX

General Motors surrendered itself to temptation in 1970 and lifted its 400-cubic-inch ban on intermediate cars. That decision unleashed some of the quickest automobiles ever to come out of Detroit and helped make 1970 the pinnacle year for American muscle. At the forefront of the rush to power was Buick. Its performance offering was again based on the midsize Skylark, which got fresh styling for '70. The GS 455 was named for its 455-cubic-inch V-8 that was rated at 350 horsepower in base trim and 360 when the Stage 1 upgrade package was ordered. Both engines put out a prodigious 510 pound-feet of torque. During the year, Buick unveiled the ultimate expression of its ultimate supercar, the GSX. It came in Apollo White or Saturn Yellow set off by unique stripes and spoilers. Only 687 GSXs were built.

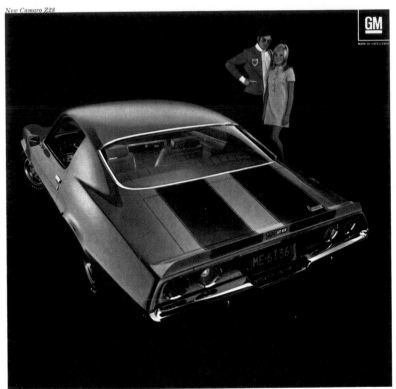

New Camaro Z28

Separates the men from the toys.

Remember when you were a kid and you put a lot of trick stuff on your bike to make it look like something it wasn't?

A lot of so-called "sporty cars" still operate that way.

But not this one.

The new Camaro Z28 is as good looking underneath as it is on top.

With a 360-horse Turbo-Fire 350 V8. And with a Hurst shifter that comes along for the ride when you order the 4-speed.

Then there's the suspension that lets you feel the road without feeling the bumps. And the quick ratio steering. And the special wheels with the F60 x 15 tires. And on, and on, and on.

But don't just take our word for it. Pick one up at your Chevy dealer's Sports Department and take it for a road test.

You'll see we're not kidding around.

Putting you first, keeps us first.

1970
Chevrolet Camaro Z28

Camaro was redesigned for 1970. It kept its 108-inch wheelbase but otherwise underwent wholesale change with a new coupe body that was an instant classic. The Z28 returned as a $573 package, the heart of which was a new engine, the Corvette's 350-cubic-inch LT-1 V-8. A timeless small block, the LT-1 was rated at 370 horsepower in the 'Vette and 360 in the Z28. A Hurst-shifted Muncie four-speed was a mandatory extra, and for the first time, an automatic was optional. Hood and decklid striping, black grille, and mag-type steel wheels were standard, as was a rear spoiler. The Z28 had matured. If it had lost some of its predecessors' juvenile zeal, it surpassed them in acceleration, balance, and refinement. *Car and Driver* called the '70 "an automobile of uncommon merit... a car of brilliant performance...."

Other cars wish the Chevelle SS 396 would hold still long enough for them to catch up.

Other cars wish the 1970 SS 396 hadn't added those 25 more horses to boost its standard V8 to 350 hp.

Other cars wish the SS 396 didn't offer you that new air-gulping Cowl Induction Hood.

Other cars wish the SS 396 didn't offer a 4-speed or a 3-range Turbo Hydra-matic transmission.

And other cars wish the stock SS 396 didn't give you power disc brakes, beefed-up suspension, F70 x 14 white-lettered wide ovals and 7"- wide sport wheels.

Aren't you glad other cars don't have anything to say about it?

On the move.

Chevelle SS 396. Other cars wish we'd keep it this way.

1970
Chevrolet Chevelle SS

The age of muscle peaked in 1970, and Chevelle was there to herald its ascent. When GM lifted its displacement ban on midsize cars, Chevy responded with a 454 V-8 that *started* at 360 horsepower and topped out at an attention-getting 450. This was muscle's summit. The wrapper was a restyled Chevelle that again presented the Super Sport as an option package for hardtops and convertibles. The new SS 454 package cost $503 and included a 360-horse 454 called the LS5. Then there was the LS6. This was the ultimate 454, with a 800-cfm Holley four-barrel on an aluminum intake, 11.25:1 compression, solid lifters, and four-bolt mains. Its 450 horsepower rating was the highest of the muscle era. *Hot Rod*'s LS6 SS 454 clipped off a 13.4-second quarter-mile at 108.7 mph.

Charger is tickled pink over its new lower price.

Even with new, slightly extra-cost Panther Pink paint, Charger is priced lower than last year. How come? Because of changes like a front bench seat instead of bucket seats. (Don't think of it as losing buckets, you're gaining an extra passenger.) And the door pockets are gone. The garnish moulding on the windows is simpler. And the electric clock is now optional. Still, Charger remains basically the Charger you remember. The shape. The hidden headlights. Racing gas cap. Full instrumentation with readably round dials. Heavy-duty suspension with calmly predictable handling. If you want the tracking any flatter, you'll have to go to Charger R/T. 1970 Dodge Charger. Our classic Super Shape . . . no matter what color it is.

Dodge CHRYSLER MOTORS CORPORATION

1970
Dodge Charger R/T SE

The Charger's basic body was in its third season, but a new chrome loop front bumper and a full-width tail-lamp housing helped freshen the look. The color palette added some youthful appeal, borrowing high-impact hues like Panther Pink and Plum Crazy from Dodge's first pony car, the Challenger. New front seats were the car's first high-back buckets, and a hip pistol-grip shifter now topped the available four-speed's Hurst shifter. For the first time, Charger could be optioned with an electric sliding sunroof. Again standard on the R/T was the 375-horsepower 440. The 425-horse Hemi remained on the option list and was joined by a 440 equipped with a trio of two-barrel carbs that was rated at 390 ponies. Rising insurance rates and tougher competition helped cause R/T sales to fall by half to 10,337.

Boss 302–The Ground Groover!

Car and Driver magazine says, "The Boss 302 may just be the new standard by which everything from Detroit must be judged."

wheels, and those great sport slats for the tinted backlite. Your biggest problem—trying not to spend 24 hours a day driving it!

For the full story on all the performance Fords for 1970, visit your Ford Dealer and get our big 16-page 1970 Performance Digest. Or write to:

FORD PERFORMANCE DIGEST, Dept. SG-16,
P.O. Box 747, Dearborn, Michigan 48121.

MUSTANG Ford

This is Ford's answer to a long, tough, twisting road—Boss 302!

Boss 302 is Ford's pavement-hugging, corner-chopping, flat-riding, curve-clinging road lover. Take it out on the snakiest, windingest track you know, stick it in third and pour on the power. The Boss'll stay with that course like a slot car sticks in its groove. It couldn't be any other way, because Boss was born on the winding, twisting, Trans-Am circuits, where specially modified Mustangs hung tighter and went quicker to win two championships. That's where we learned how to set up a car like the Boss.

The standard specs sound like a $9000 European sports job instead of a reliable, reasonably priced American pony car. Start with a front spoiler; then, under the black hood—Ford's F.I.A. sanctioned 5-litre V-8; next a fully synchronized 4-speed that's butter smooth and shifts knife-quick with a T-handle Hurst Shifter*. Control is precise with 16 to 1 manual steering, and the Boss stops right now thanks to floating-caliper power front disc brakes.

Rear axle is heavy-duty 3.5:1 with staggered shocks to combat wheel hop. Suspension is firm, sway-resisting competition type, of course. We glue the whole package to the deck with F60-15 superwide, belted bias-ply tires. Wheels are wide rim with chrome trim rings.

Don't be shy about taking the Boss to your local drag strip. That precision-cast jewel of a lightweight V-8 will move you out for a real quick quarter mile. It's a deep-breathing high winder—290 horsepower at 5800 from just 302 cubes! New heads with giant ports and canted valves — 2.19" intakes, 1.71" exhausts — do the trick.

The standard Boss is so complete, about all you need to do is think about options like Magnum 500 chrome

1970
Ford Mustang Boss 302

Ford's answer to the Camaro Z28 was the Boss 302. Like the Chevy, it was built to qualify Trans Am racing versions and used a fortified 302-cubic-inch four-barrel V-8 rated at 290 horsepower. The Boss 302 launched for 1969 and returned for '70 in greater numbers. All Boss 302s had stiffened underpinnings and did away with the regular Mustang fastback's fake bodyside scoops. A rear spoiler and flip-up rear-window slats were optional. Blackout trim and stripes completed the look. A Hurst-shifted four-speed was mandatory. The '70 had single headlamps flanked by simulated vents and could be ordered with a functional shaker scoop that mounted to the air cleaner and quivered with the engine. In Trans Am competition, racing Boss 302s retook the 1970 crown from Chevy. Street versions weren't always as quick as a 302-powered Z28, but they cornered better and had a less-peaky, more flexible engine.

Torino: Winner of Motor Trend's "Car of the Year" Competition

Wherever they talk about ET's that's where you'll see Cobra Ram-Air 429's with Drag Packs — winning!

Torino Cobra: Look for it in the Winner's Circle!

The Cobra's one very big reason that Torino won Motor Trend's "Car of the Year" Award for 1970. Torinos (Motor Trend named the whole line) won out over the newest and best the competition had to offer.

Cobra is the top performer: It puts a lot of "go" power in your driveway at a very reasonable price. The standard powerplant is a 360-hp 429-cubic-inch V-8. But that's only the beginning. The standard Cobra package also includes a 4-speed fully synchronized manual transmission with trigger-quick Hurst Shifter®.

The standard chassis is all performance, too. Competition suspension, of course, with ultra-high rate front and rear springs, staggered shocks and heavy-duty stabilizer bar. To keep Cobra in the groove when the going gets tricky we nail it down with 7-in. rim wheels and F70-14 wide-tread belted tires with raised white lettering.

One of the major reasons for the Motor Trend award, other than style, quality, performance, and handling was Torino's "broad range of choice" and Cobra's no exception.

There are two great optional 429 V-8's. Brand new for 1970 are the high-output jobs with newly designed heads, larger valves and ports, high lift cam, dual header-type exhaust, high-riser manifold, the works. They rate at 370 hp. Top engine is the 429 Cobra Jet 4V Ram-Air V-8 that gives you extra power when you need it.

Like to win at your local drag strip? Order a Cobra with the 429 Drag Pack: No-spin differential, 4.30 to 1 ratio, engine oil cooler, forged aluminum pistons, and 4-bolt center main caps.

Torino Cobra—in your Ford Dealer's Performance Corner . . . one of the most powerful reasons for Torino's "Car of the Year" award!

Cobra Power Teams

ENGINE	COMPRESSION RATIO	HORSEPOWER RPM	TORQUE
429 4V V-8	10.5 to 1	360 hp @ 4600 rpm	480 lb.
429 4V Cobra V-8	11.3 to 1	370 hp @ 5400 rpm	450 lb.
429 4V Cobra Jet Ram-Air V-8	11.3 to 1	370 hp @ 5400 rpm	450 lb.

4-speed fully synchronized manual transmission standard, SelectShift automatic optional.

For the full story on all the performance Fords for 1970, visit your Ford Dealer and get our big 16-page 1970 Performance Digest. Or write to:

FORD PERFORMANCE DIGEST, Dept. HR-24
P.O. Box 747, Dearborn, Michigan 48121.

COBRA

PRE-STAGED
STAGED

The new shape of winning muscle on America's drag strips this year.

1970
Ford Torino Cobra

Judging from their newfound plumpness, Detroit's 1970 crop of intermediates were not only midsized, but middle-aged. Nowhere was that more true than at Ford, where the Torino gained an inch of wheelbase and five full inches of length, making it one of the largest cars in the segment. At least the reshaped sheetmetal looked aero-inspired. Replacing the willing but aged 428-cubic-inch mill was a new 429-cube V-8. This was not the Boss 429, but a fresh design with thin-wall construction and canted-valve heads. Ford retained a familiar moniker for the hottest model, the Torino Cobra. The standard engine was a 360-horsepower version of the 429. Things quickly got serious with a 370-horse variant. With the available shaker scoop, this engine was dubbed the 429 Cobra Jet Ram-Air, but horsepower stayed at 370.

New Cougar Eliminator. Password for action.
Spoilers hold it down. Nothing holds it back.

You're looking at raw muscle. Muscle straining for the kind of action you want. The Eliminator sports aerodynamic spoilers front and rear. A standard 351-4V kicks up 300 hp. Optional powerplants include a high-output "Boss" 302-4V with mechanical lifters and the CJ 428-4V. Standard features include: high-performance axle ratios, hood scoop, rally clock, tach, black-out grille. Optional 4-speed Hurst Shifter.³ Everything you need to take on the competition. Cougar Eliminator from Mercury, password for action in the 70's.

'70 Mercury Cougar Eliminator

MERCURY COUGAR Ford

1970
Mercury Cougar Eliminator

Cougar played the suave big brother to the rambunc-
tious Mustang, but given the right motivation, the cat
had claws. Mercury introduced its sporty coupe in 1967
as a luxury-touring alternative to the pony-car herd. It
had mature styling and upscale interior appointments
and was built on a Mustang chassis stretched three
inches to provide a longer, ride-enhancing wheelbase.
Cougar's performance profile was raised in April '69 with
the introduction of the Eliminator package. Cougar was
mildly restyled for 1970, and the Eliminator returned for
its final season. A 300-horsepower 351 was standard, the
290-horse Boss 302 or 335-hp 428 Cobra Jet optional.
The standard hood scoop was only functional when ram
air was ordered. A blackout grille, side stripes, and front
and rear spoilers enhanced the look.

New Cyclone Spoiler. Password for action. You'd better bring along a drag chute.

Here's the muscle machine that puts wind to work for you. Tested out at 100 mph, front spoiler drops lift from 186 to 120.5 pounds. Rear spoiler cuts it down from 67.5 to a flat, fast 5.8. The Cyclone Spoiler comes equipped with all basic competition hardware. CJ 429 V-8 (370 hp) force-fed by ram-air induction. Four-speed Hurst Shifter.* The works. Get on top of the action with Cyclone Spoiler from Mercury, password for action in the 70's. Just see your Lincoln-Mercury dealer.

MERCURY CYCLONE *Ford*

'70 Mercury Cyclone Spoiler

1970
Mercury Cyclone Spoiler

The 1970 Cyclone Spoiler might be Mercury's best-ever performance car. The body was finally unique from that of the fastback Fords, and its Coke-bottle shape had an individualized flavor. The Spoiler actually came better equipped for battle than its Ford Torino Cobra cousin. The standard mill was the 370-horsepower ram-air 429 V-8. A Hurst-stirred four-speed and a Traction-Lok rear end completed the drivetrain, with an automatic transmission optional. Spoiler didn't use a shaker hood, going instead with an integrated functional scoop. A chin spoiler and rear air foil were also included, while exterior adornment was left to simple tape stripes and one of six "Competition" colors. Befitting a Mercury, the Cyclone Spoiler was a *big* car. It shared Torino's wheelbase, but its body was nearly four inches longer.

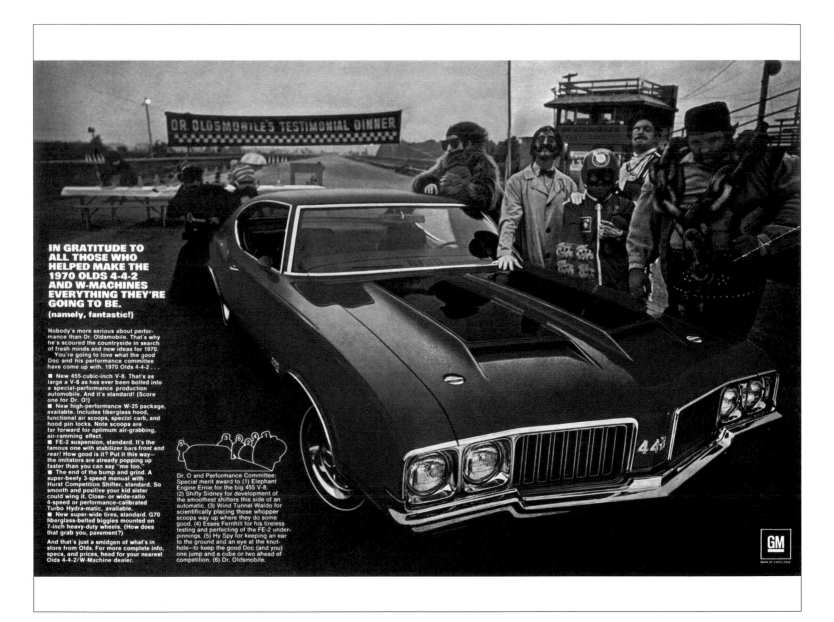

IN GRATITUDE TO ALL THOSE WHO HELPED MAKE THE 1970 OLDS 4-4-2 AND W-MACHINES EVERYTHING THEY'RE GOING TO BE.
(namely, fantastic!)

Nobody's more serious about performance than Dr. Oldsmobile. That's why he's scoured the countryside in search of fresh minds and new ideas for 1970. You're going to love what the good Doc and his performance committee have come up with. 1970 Olds 4-4-2 . . .

■ New 455-cubic-inch V-8. That's as large a V-8 as has ever been bolted into a special-performance production automobile. And it's standard! (Score one for Dr. O!)
■ New high-performance W-25 package, available. Includes fiberglass hood, functional air scoops, special carb, and hood pin locks. Note scoops are far forward for optimum air-grabbing, air-ramming effect.
■ FE-2 suspension, standard. It's the famous one with stabilizer bars *front and rear!* How good is it? Put it this way— the imitators are already popping up faster than you can say "me too."
■ The end of the bump and grind. A super-beefy 3-speed manual with Hurst Competition Shifter, standard. So smooth and positive your kid sister could wing it. Close- or wide-ratio 4-speed or performance-calibrated Turbo Hydra-matic, available.
■ New super-wide tires, standard. G70 fiberglass-belted biggies mounted on 7-inch heavy-duty wheels. (How does that grab you, pavement?)

And that's just a smidgen of what's in store from Olds. For more complete info, specs, and prices, head for your nearest Olds 4-4-2/W-Machine dealer.

Dr. O and Performance Committee: Special merit award to (1) Elephant Engine Ernie for the big 455 V-8. (2) Shifty Sidney for development of the smoothest shifters this side of an automatic. (3) Wind Tunnel Waldo for scientifically placing those whopper scoops way up where they do some good. (4) Esses Fernhill for his tireless testing and perfecting of the FE-2 under-pinnings. (5) Hy Spy for keeping an ear to the ground and an eye at the knot-hole—to keep the good Doc (and you) one jump and a cube or two ahead of competition. (6) Dr. Oldsmobile.

GM
MARK OF EXCELLENCE

114

1970
Oldsmobile 4-4-2

For 1970, Oldsmobile introduced perhaps the best all-around 4-4-2 ever. The major advance was the newly standard 455-cubic-inch V-8, an under-stressed, big-port engine with tug-boat torque. Although larger in displacement, it also had an advanced design that kept its exterior dimensions compact and its weight below that of 1969's 400-cube V-8. It made 365 horsepower in base form, an underrated 370 in W-30 guise. A Hurst-managed four speed or a performance-calibrated Turbo 400 automatic with a Hurst Dual-Gate shifter were the transmission options. The W-30 package also included a fiberglass hood with functional scoops, plastic inner fenders, and less sound deadener than other 4-4-2s. Oldsmobile's 1970 W-30s blended a plush cabin with athletic road manners and vivid acceleration. It was the thinking-man's approach to muscle.

Everybody offers a car.
Only Plymouth offers a system.

Heck, anybody can build cars with big engines. Plymouth's Rapid Transit System is a lot more than that.

As the name implies, it's a system; a total concept in transportation that goes far beyond eight pistons and a steering wheel.

The Rapid Transit System is racing—at Daytona, Riverside, Cecil County—and the race cars themselves—Dragsters, Super Stocks, Oval Stockers—the essence of high-performance machinery.

The Rapid Transit System is information —the straight scoop from Plymouth to you —tips on how to tune your car, modify it, which equipment to use, and how to set the whole thing up for racing. For a free brochure on all that's available, just write *Rapid Transit System—Dept. A, P.O. Box 7749, Detroit, Mich. 48231.*

The System is person-to-person contact —us and you—at Supercar Clinics conducted throughout the country by our own racers.

The System is high-performance parts— now conveniently packaged and available through your Plymouth dealer.

Above all, the R.T.S. is the product— everything from a Valiant Duster 340, all the way to a Hemi-'Cuda with a quivering Air Grabber. Each car in the System is a *complete* high-performance car, with suspension, brakes, driveline and tires to match.

Compare Plymouth's Rapid Transit System with mere cars.

And if you can't beat it—join it.

1970
Plymouth 'Cuda

The restyled 1970 Plymouth Barracuda may have looked lean, but with the right engine, it could be very mean. Sporting derivations again were called 'Cudas and featured five hot V-8s, from the sharp 275-horsepower 340 to the merciless 425-horse 426 Hemi. Plymouth knew the mission and gave Hemi 'Cudas a suspension tailored to heavy-metal acceleration. There wasn't a rear stabilizer bar, but the rear leaf springs numbered five on the right, six on the left, with thicknesses chosen to equalize tire loads during hole shots. Wheel hop was negligible, but careless starts would send the tires up in smoke. The 'Cuda's standard hood had phony intakes, but a functional shaker hood scoop was included with the Hemi and optional on other 'Cudas. For 1970, Hemi 'Cuda production totaled 652 hardtops and 14 convertibles.

The obvious reason
Richard Petty came back.

1970
Plymouth Superbird

On the high-banked ovals of the stock car racing circuit, the "aero-wars" between Chrysler and Ford produced the most outrageous cars of the muscle era. Dodge had the "winged warrior" Charger Daytona for 1969, and Plymouth's version debuted for 1970. The Road Runner Superbird had a special nose cone fitted to the front fenders and a lengthened hood lifted from the 1970 Dodge Coronet. All production Superbirds wore vinyl tops to hide the welding seams left when the flush-mounted rear window was fitted. And in case a car with a huge rear wing and a wind-tunnel-shaped snout was too subtle, Plymouth added cartoon Road Runner graphics, flat-black panels on the nose cone, and billboard-size "Plymouth" stickers to the rear flanks. There were three engine choices: a 375-horsepower 440, 390-horse "440+6" with triple two-barrels, or the 426 Hemi.

Introducing a sensible alternative to the money-squeezing, insurance-strangling muscle cars of America.
The Hornet SC/360.

The Hornet SC/360 lists for only $2,663¹. Which is surprising when you consider what the September issue of Motor Trend had to say about it:

The SC/360 is just a plain gas to drive. It has lightning quick performance...It handles like a dream, especially on the TransAm road course at Michigan International Speedway where we had an opportunity to test it.

A 360 CID V-8 engine with 245 horsepower is standard.

So is a 3-on-the-floor, all synchromesh transmission. A heavy-duty clutch. D70 x 14 Polyglas™ tires. 14 x 6 mag style wheels. Space saver spare. Rally stripe. And individual reclining seats.

To make it even gutsier, the SC/360 also comes with a long list of options.

Among which you'll find a 4-barrel 360 V-8 that develops 285 horsepower. An all synchro 4-on-the-floor with Hurst shifter. Ram air induction with hood scoop. 3.54 or 3.91 rear axle with Twin-Grip. Dual exhausts. White letter tires. Heavy-duty suspension. And a big tach.

But even with the added cost of these options, the SC/360 ends up with a lower list price than most of its bigger, muscle-bound competitors.

And because of its standard 12.5:1 weight-to-power ratio, insurance on the SC/360 ends up lower, too.

As a leading car magazine has said, "The day of the heavy 400-cube, 400-horsepower supercar may be just about over."

Manufacturer's suggested retail price. Federal taxes included. State and local taxes, if any, destination charges excluded.

If you had to compete with GM, Ford and Chrysler what would you do? ▟▆ **American Motors**

1971
AMC Hornet SC/360

After peaking in 1970, the era of muscle was entering twilight by 1971. AMC's new compact, the Hornet, debuted for '70, and the two-door sedan was a reasonable basis for a low-profile performance offering for 1971. The Hornet SC/360 packed a 360-cubic-inch V-8 with a two-barrel carb and a modest 245 horsepower in standard form. A $199 "Go" package included a four-barrel and a ram-air setup for a more satisfying 285 ponies. A three-speed manual was standard, with a Hurst-stirred four-speed or an automatic optional. An SC/360 could turn high 14s in the quarter with the four-speed. That wasn't enough to run with the big-cube holdovers, but the car did combine reasonable quickness with a taut suspension to make it a pleasing handler. Starting at just $2663, only 784 were built in the SC/360's lone model year.

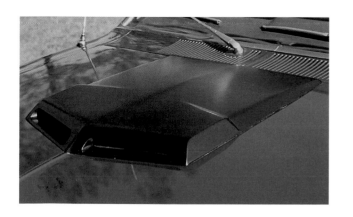

CHARGER R/T
This car was designed strictly for adults.

A Charger R/T doesn't need anything but the shape it's in to tell you what it is. The king.

The one that has the whole job done right.

Check the credentials. 440 Magnum, dual exhausts, bright tips.

Full instrumentation.

Extra-heavy-duty suspension.

The automatic that can take it is standard, three-speed TorqueFlite.

The buckets have built-in head restraints. The dash has simulated wood-grained panels. The windshield wipers are hidden. Concealed headlights are optional. So is a little device that washes them with a brush.

Still, it's the way it all goes together that counts. Balance. The extra leaf in the right rear spring to handle the torque. Easily adjustable torsion bars, heavy-duty brakes. Don't worry about it. You get 'em. Standard.

STANDARD EQUIPMENT

440 Magnum V8 □ Performance hood with blackout treatment □ Ventless door glass (43" radius) □ Glove box lamp and lock □ 150-mph speedometer □ Full instrumentation with fuel, temperature, alternator and oil pressure gauges □ Cigarette lighter □

Heater/windshield defroster with 3-speed fan □ Simulated wood-grained door and instrument panel trim inserts □ Color-keyed carpeting □ Vinyl bucket seats with integral head restraints □ Transistorized regulator □ TorqueFlite automatic transmission □ Extra-heavy-duty suspension (includes high-rate torsion bars, heavy-duty shock absorbers, extra-heavy-duty rear springs with special right rear spring, and sway bar) □ Heavy-duty brakes: 11" x 3", front; 11" x 2½", rear □ G70x14 wide-tread, raised white letter, bias-belted tires □ Dual exhausts.

CHARGER Super Bee
Even with a 383 Magnum...it's a regular gas.

Hey, man. It's easy to own a super set of wheels if you have a super budget to feed it with. Check?

On the other hand, if you think about it for a while, maybe you could find another place to use the green. If you had some left over. And here's how you get it.

Super Bee, the great-looking piece of man's iron that knows how to live on a budget. Start with a 383 Magnum that's learned to like regular. Plus a power-to-weight ratio that combines handling, stopping, and the ability to leave quickly. Add heavy-duty suspension, super brakes, F70 x 14 bias-

belted skins, and the floor-mounted full-synchro three-speed. That's some motor.

And boy, is it great when you have enough left over to take it out Saturday nights. There are a lot of nice, good-thinking reasons to buy a Super Bee. So ignore the fact that it looks like tomorrow and runs like it's all down hill.

Sure you will.

STANDARD EQUIPMENT

383 Magnum V8 (uses regular fuel) □ Performance hood with blackout treatment □ Ventless door glass (43"

radius) □ Simulated wood-grained door trim panel inserts, instrument panel applique and Rallye Instrument Cluster with 150-mph speedometer and oil pressure gauge □ Heater/windshield defroster with 3-speed fan □ Carpeting □ Rallye Suspension Package (includes heavy-duty torsion bars, heavy-duty rear springs, sway bar, and heavy-duty shock absorbers) □ 3-speed fully synchronized transmission with floor shift □ Heavy-duty brakes: 11" x 3", front; 11" x 2½", rear □ F70x14 wide-tread, white sidewall, bias-belted tires □ Dual exhausts.

Styled road wheel with chromed trim ring   Ramcharger hood   Tachometer   Racing mirror   Bright exhaust tips   Rallye wheel and E60 tire   Pistol grip

1971
Dodge Charger

The 1971 Charger was a radical departure from its pre-
decessor, losing two inches of wheelbase and gaining
Coke-bottle contours. The R/T remained the performance leader, though now it shared its body with the
Super Bee. R/T versions stayed true to their roots with
a daunting underhood lineup. The 370-horsepower
440 Magnum was standard, with the 385-horse 440 Six
Pack available at extra cost. Topping the lineup was the
Hemi. Non-Hemi R/Ts like this one came standard with
nonfunctional hood louvers. A blackout hood graphic,
tape stripes, Rallye wheels, and special door skins with
simulated air extractors rounded out the R/T appearance
features. High-impact colors and spoilers on the rear
deck and chin were optional. Charger R/T sales totaled
just 3118 for the year.

There are two kinds of **Barracudas in this world.**
Those that do **...and those that really do.**

On the left you see one of Plymouth's super-tough 1971 'Cudas. A 340 cubic incher.

We recommend the 'Cuda 340 for those of you who tend to prefer the merits of a lightweight, high-winding engine . . . for those of you who are well aware that Swede Savage is not a Swede . . . and for those of you who just simply won't be happy with anything less than a for-real sporty car.

Like all 'Cudas, the 'Cuda 340 possesses an in-credibly well engineered underside. ('Cudas carry virtually the same brawny chassis setup as our intermediate-size Supercars.)

Heavy-duty torsion bars, rear shock absorbers, rear springs, ball joints, front and rear anti-sway bars and brakes all come standard.

Now then, for you hard core straight-liners out there, there's the car on the right, and its legendary engine to consider—the Hemi-'Cuda.

Hemi-'Cudas come with *extra*-heavy-duty (what else) torsion bars, shock absorbers, rear springs and rear axle. As do our 440 6-barrel 'Cudas.

There is, of course, another way to go.

You can order a 1971 Barracuda and the good stuff (like fat tires, trick wheels and heavy-duty suspension) with a 225 cubic inch Six! Or 318 V-8. Or the 383 2-barrel V-8 engine.

So, in other words, you can order a 'Cuda from the Rapid Transit System—or its first cousin from our stable of Barracudas.

For some time now, Plymouth has offered the car enthusiasts of this country the most comprehensive selection of high-performance cars available.

And we still do.

The Rapid Transit System. Coming through.

1971
Plymouth 'Cuda

Chrysler's 1970 pony cars were muscle styling master-pieces, with crisp long-hood/short-deck proportions and a wide, sinister stance. For '71, Barracudas got revised taillights and a busy grille with quad headlights and six "venturi" air inlets. The performance-oriented 'Cuda variants amped up the ostentation with hood pins, chrome front fender "gills," twin-scooped hood, and a host of "look-at-me" options. Popular add-ons included the shaker hood scoop, rear spoiler, and wild "billboard" bodyside stripes that called out engine size. For the time being, there was still plenty of go to match all this show. 'Cudas again featured 340, 383, 440, and 426 Hemi power, though the 440 was now available only in six-barrel form. Still, it was clear by the end of 1971 that the 'Cuda was a fish out of water. Barracuda sales plummeted 66 percent for the model year as the pony car market waned.

In case you haven't noticed, Pontiac's '73 Firebirds are here.

We build four different kinds. For people who take driving excitement seriously. The question is...how serious do you want to get?

Trans Am: As serious as they come.
It's the red one above. See how serious it is? Everything functional. The spoilers spoil. The air dams dam. That's why a lot of folks rank it as the best performing Yank on the road.

A 455, 4-bbl. V-8 with a 4-speed manual is standard. So is fast-rate variable-ratio power steering. Power front disc brakes. And a very firm suspension.

No, the giant bird on the hood isn't functional. It's not standard, either. You have to order it. But...!

Formula: Two scoops, three flavors.
The two scoops you can see on the hood above. The flavors are a 350 V-8, a 400 V-8, a 455 V-8. Order the Formula 'Bird as you see fit.

The new interior is all business.

So are the standard front disc brakes and the handling package you can order.

While the scoops look tough, the toughest part of any Firebird is the front bumper. It's made of Endura to help fight dents and dings. And it's been reinforced this year to make it stronger.

Esprit: Can a sports car be luxurious?
Esprit wipes out all doubt. The new bucket seats, the new cloth or all-vinyl upholstery, the new instrument panel and door trim are as plush as you'll find in many a luxury car.

The ride's almost that plush, too.

Basic Firebird: What we didn't sacrifice for price.
This is our easiest to own Firebird.

You still get molded foam bucket seats; loop-pile carpeting; High-Low ventilation; the Endura bumper; a strong, double-shell roof that absorbs sound; Firebird's futuristic styling and outstanding handling.

That's our way with sports cars. Are you ready to get serious?

Buckle up for safety. Pontiac Motor Division

The Wide-Track people have a way with cars.

1973
Pontiac Firebird Formula

Firebirds were still wearing the basic look introduced for 1970, and performance-minded buyers remained able to chose from Formula and Trans Am models. The muscle era was winding down by 1973, but that didn't stop Pontiac from introducing a new Super-Duty 455 engine. Initially rated at a whopping 310 *net* horsepower, most SD-455 engines actually packed a milder camshaft and put out 290 ponies. Among other goodies, the SD-455 had a stronger block, four-bolt main bearings, forged rods, TRW pistons, and a provision for dry-sump lubrication. A Firebird running the SD-455 engine could accelerate to 60 mph in less than 5.5 seconds and run the quarter-mile in as little as 13.8 seconds, even with automatic—astounding for this era of declining performance. In 1973, only 43 Formula Firebirds were fitted with the Super Duty 455.